Under The Sun

Why Nothing Matters (And Why That's Okay)

Aham Igbokwe

Under the Sun: Why Nothing Matters (And Why That's Okay)
by Aham Igbokwe

Disclaimer

This book is intended for general informational and reflective purposes only.
It does not constitute professional advice of any kind, including but not limited to medical, psychological, legal, financial, or pastoral counselling.

The views and perspectives expressed are those of the author and are offered as observations on human experience, culture, and meaning. Readers are encouraged to exercise their own judgment and discernment and to seek appropriate professional advice where necessary.

Notes on Sources and Interpretation

This work draws on a range of historical, philosophical, psychological, and cultural sources. Any resemblance to particular individuals, living or deceased, is coincidental or based on composite or illustrative examples.

References to research, studies, or historical material are provided for context and reflection, not as definitive or exhaustive treatment of those subjects.

ISBN (Paperback): 978-1-918518-10-8
ISBN (eBook): 978-1-918518-11-5

First edition
Printed in the United Kingdom

Cover design: @IamPastorAham
Interior design and typesetting: @IamPastorAham

Epigraph

"The trouble with the world is not that people know too little,
but that they know so many things that aren't so."
— Mark Twain

Contents

Chapter 1: Why Success Doesn't Settle the Soul

The week before David Remnick became editor of *The New Yorker*, he remembers feeling the exact emotion he'd spent fifteen years chasing: arrival. He'd worked his way up through journalism's brutalist hierarchy—police beat, foreign correspondent, Pulitzer winner. Now he had the job. The corner office. The institutional authority he'd imagined would feel like vindication.

It didn't.

He described the sensation years later as "a hole where satisfaction was supposed to be." Not depression, exactly. Not regret. Just an odd, persistent awareness that the reward didn't transform him the way he'd expected. He was still himself. Still restless. Still uncertain whether any of it mattered the way he'd told himself it would.

The feeling lasted about three days before he went back to work.

The strange thing about success is not that it disappoints people.

The strange thing is how predictably it does—and how surprised we still act every time.

Most people don't describe it as disappointment at first. They describe it as confusion. A quiet, awkward sense that something didn't happen the way it was supposed to.

They did the work.
They made the sacrifices.
They reached the goal.

And yet, something inside them stayed restless.

At best, success gives you a short-lived sense of relief—like scratching an itch that immediately moves somewhere else.

You achieve the thing.
You pause.
You look around.

And then your mind starts asking, *Is this it?*

That question is more common than people admit. It just doesn't show up on LinkedIn.

So instead of talking about it, we double down. We raise the stakes. We tell ourselves the problem wasn't success—it was *insufficient* success. We didn't go far enough. Didn't aim high enough. Didn't optimise hard enough.

The chase resumes.

This is how people end up exhausted by lives they once dreamed of having.

We live in a culture that treats achievement like a moral category. Win, and you're virtuous. Lose, and you clearly didn't want it badly enough. Productivity becomes character. Busyness becomes evidence. Visibility becomes worth.

Everything turns into a scoreboard.

And scoreboards never sleep.

The architecture of modern life depends on this equation. Our platforms reward output. Our institutions measure contribution. Our social rituals revolve around professional identity. When someone asks what you *do*, they're really asking what you've *achieved*—and by extension, what you're worth.

This isn't unique to capitalism, technology, or any particular economic system. It's older than that. Humans have always competed for status. What's newer is how completely we've fused status with meaning.

Achievement used to be one source of worth among many—family, craft, community, faith. Now it's often the only one we trust. Everything else feels optional. Success feels mandatory.

The stakes quietly escalate.

A promotion isn't just a promotion—it's proof you're progressing.
A platform isn't just a platform—it's proof you have something to say.
A title isn't just a title—it's proof you haven't wasted your time.

We've turned work into an existential proving ground. And proving grounds don't offer rest—they offer the next test.

The strange thing is that almost everyone eventually notices the same pattern, even if they describe it differently: **achievement moves the furniture around, but it doesn't change the room.**

New title. Same anxiety.
New salary. Same restlessness.
New audience. Same self-doubt.

This isn't cynicism. It's repetition.

Watch people long enough, and you'll see it everywhere—the quiet confusion that creeps in after the applause fades. A sense that the reward didn't quite justify the cost. The discomfort of realising that the ladder you climbed so carefully doesn't actually lean against anything permanent.

We pretend this is a modern problem, but it isn't. Humans have been reaching the top and feeling underwhelmed for as long as there have been tops to reach. Alexander wept when there were no more worlds to conquer—not because he failed, but because victory didn't feel like he thought it would. The journals of high achievers across centuries share a familiar refrain: *I got there. And then what?*

What *is* modern is how aggressively we deny it.

We sell success as salvation.
We market ambition as identity.
We treat achievement as if it's supposed to answer questions it was never designed to address.

Who am I?
Did my life mean anything?
Was this worth it?

Success can't answer those.

So, we keep interrogating it anyway.

That's where the disappointment comes from—not from failure, but from misplaced expectations.

Social researchers have been documenting this for years. Once basic needs are met, additional success brings rapidly diminishing emotional returns. Satisfaction spikes briefly, then settles back to baseline. We adapt. We normalise. What once felt extraordinary becomes routine. The relief expires faster than expected. Psychologists call this hedonic adaptation—the mechanism by which humans return to emotional equilibrium regardless of external circumstances.[1] Lottery winners report temporary euphoria, then revert to prior happiness levels within months. The same pattern holds for career advancement, recognition, and wealth accumulation. The system is designed to stabilise, not to escalate.

This isn't ingratitude.
It's how humans are wired.

But when an entire culture builds its sense of meaning on achievement, this wiring becomes a problem. Motion turns into necessity. Stopping feels dangerous. Slowing down feels irresponsible. Rest starts to feel like a character flaw.

Life becomes an ongoing performance review with no closing date.

And the cost quietly accumulates: anxiety disguised as ambition, burnout disguised as dedication, identity reduced to output. We chase the feeling we had the first time we succeeded, not realising that the feeling was never about the success itself—it was about novelty, about relief from uncertainty, about the brief dopamine hit of crossing a finish line. The second time, the third time, the hundredth time—the hit weakens. The finish line moves.

But we don't stop running.

We tell ourselves the problem is execution. Strategy. Discipline. Anything but the premise itself.

Here's the uncomfortable truth beneath all of it:

Success doesn't fail because it gives too little.
It fails because we ask it for too much.

We expect permanence from temporary things.
We expect identity from outcomes.
We expect meaning to arrive on a schedule.

When it doesn't, we assume something has gone wrong—with us, or with the process. Rarely do we consider that the expectation itself may be the problem.

The assumption that achievement will finally settle the restlessness inside you is not a personal failing. It's a cultural inheritance. We've been taught to believe that *enough* success will eventually produce *enough* peace. That the proper promotion, the right project, and the correct recognition will complete something essential. The problem is *how much* we've achieved, not *what we're asking achievement to do.*

But achievement was never designed to bear that weight.

It can provide relief, pride, even joy. It can open doors. It can prove competence. It can fund security.

What it cannot do is justify your existence.
What it cannot do is settle your soul.

This realisation unsettles people. If success won't settle the soul, then what will?

But that question rushes ahead too quickly.

The more critical shift happens earlier: when you stop demanding that achievement justify your existence, it loosens its grip on you. You can still work hard without believing your worth is on trial. You can still aim high without pretending the outcome will complete you. You can still enjoy success without turning it into a verdict on your life.

Work becomes work again—not worship.
Rest becomes permissible.
Failure becomes survivable.
Success becomes pleasant, not sacred.

This doesn't make life grander or simpler.

It makes it lighter.

There's a peculiar freedom in accepting that no amount of achievement will ever feel like enough—because *enough* was always the wrong metric. Enough for what? To prove what? To whom?

Once you stop trying to extract existential security from professional outcomes, the outcomes themselves become less tyrannical. You can pursue them without needing them to redeem you. You can fail at them without it meaning you failed *as a person*. You can succeed at them without the hollow confusion that follows when the high fades and you're still you.

The restlessness doesn't disappear.

But it stops masquerading as a productivity problem.

Under the sun, nothing stays impressed for very long. Not reputations. Not accomplishments. Not legacies. Time has a way of levelling the field quietly and without drama.

The executive who restructured the company retires, and within five years, no one remembers the restructuring. The artist who dominated a decade becomes a footnote in the next one. The entrepreneur who built an empire watches it dissolve or evolve into something unrecognisable. It all fades—not because it wasn't real, but because nothing under the sun resists erosion indefinitely.

Strangely, accepting that doesn't drain life of significance.

It relocates it.

Meaning stops living in the future, where success is promised to arrive eventually. It returns to the present—where effort, enjoyment, limitation, and uncertainty coexist without pretending to resolve one another.

You can work hard today not because it will finally make you whole, but because the work itself has texture and dignity. You can rest without guilt because rest doesn't threaten your value. You can fail without catastrophizing because your identity isn't on trial. You can succeed without the quiet panic that it still doesn't feel like you thought it would.

This is not a resignation.

It's calibration.

Success was never meant to settle the soul.

Once you stop asking it to, you're finally free to live—not as a résumé in progress, but as a human being passing through a temporary world.

Under the sun, that may not be everything we hoped for.

But it is enough to begin.

Chapter 2: Why "Progress" Keeps Repeating Itself

In 1995, Nicholas Negroponte published *Being Digital* and predicted that the internet would eliminate nationalism, dissolve corporate hierarchies, and create a new era of human understanding. Information would flow freely. Geographic barriers would collapse. People would connect across cultures without the friction of physical distance or institutional gatekeeping.

He wasn't naive. He was observing genuine technical capabilities and extrapolating logically.

By twenty-five years later, the internet had indeed dissolved specific barriers—and then rebuilt them in different forms. Borders became digital. Hierarchies became algorithmic. Gatekeeping became distributed but no less powerful. Instead of eliminating tribalism, platforms optimised it. Instead of fostering understanding, they monetised outrage.

Negroponte's predictions weren't wrong about what the technology could do.

They were wrong about what people would do with it.

Every generation believes it is standing at the edge of something unprecedented.

New technology.
New values.
New freedoms.
New problems—finally solvable.

We tell ourselves this time is different. We always have.

Look closely, and you'll notice a pattern: the confidence usually peaks just before the disillusionment sets in.

This is not because progress is imaginary. It's because progress is uneven. It accelerates in tools while remaining stubbornly slow in people. We build faster machines, more intelligent systems, more efficient networks—and then use them to replay the same human impulses in higher definition.

The wrapping changes.
The instincts don't.

History is full of moments that felt like turning points at the time. The printing press was supposed to end ignorance. The telegraph was meant to collapse distance and prevent misunderstanding. Radio would unify nations. Television would educate the masses. The internet would democratise truth. Social media would connect us.

Each innovation delivered something real.
Each one also exposed something unchanged.

Knowledge increased.
Wisdom did not keep pace.

If this sounds cynical, it isn't. It's descriptive.

Progress works brilliantly at expanding capacity. It is far less effective at refining desire. We become more powerful long before we become more restrained. The result is not transformation, but amplification.

Media theorist Neil Postman spent decades documenting this pattern. Technology, he argued, doesn't create new human behaviours—it scales existing ones. [1] Platforms don't invent vanity—they optimise it. Algorithms don't create outrage—they reward it. Devices don't steal attention—they monetise what we already struggle to manage.

The tools evolve.
The tendencies repeat.

You can see this most clearly in how quickly optimism turns into fatigue. New systems arrive with promises of liberation—from labour, from hierarchy, from boredom, from loneliness. Then the trade-offs surface. Efficiency breeds expectation. Convenience breeds dependence. Connection breeds comparison.

And the cycle begins again.

What makes this exhausting is not that progress fails, but that it keeps succeeding in the wrong places. We gain speed without direction. Access without discernment. Choice without satisfaction.

So, we respond the only way we know how: we accelerate.

When things don't feel better, we assume we need more innovation, more disruption, more reform. We rarely consider that repetition may be the point—not because nothing changes, but because something essential doesn't.

This is why history can sound familiar when you read it closely. Different names, different costumes, same anxieties. Power still corrupts. Wealth still concentrates. Injustice persists. Hope still rises. Disappointment still follows.

Empires rise convinced they've learned from the past. They felt surprised by how little they actually did.

The Roman Empire believed its legal systems and engineering prowess had transcended the petty tribal conflicts of earlier civilisations. Its citizens enjoyed infrastructure, entertainment, and relative stability—luxuries that previous generations could hardly imagine. Yet Rome still crumbled under the weight of corruption, overextension, and internal decay. The technology was Roman. The collapse was human.

The British Empire made similar claims in the 19th century. Railways. Telegraph networks. Global trade. Surely this time, rational administration and technological superiority would prevent the cyclical rise and fall of previous empires. But colonialism didn't eliminate exploitation—it industrialised it. Progress in logistics didn't prevent moral regression.

The pattern isn't about whether these civilisations achieved real things. They did. The pattern is about what they believed those achievements would exempt them from.

The modern world struggles with this idea because it clashes with our self-image. We prefer narratives of linear improvement. We like to believe we are moving somewhere—upward, forward, better. Cycles feel regressive. Repetition feels like failure.

But repetition is not failure.
It is a revelation.

It tells us where change is superficial and where it is stubbornly resisted. It exposes the difference between upgrading systems and transforming character.

We can build systems that process information faster, distribute resources more efficiently, and connect people more broadly. What we can't engineer is restraint, wisdom, or contentment. Those remain stubbornly manual. They require cultivation, not optimisation. And cultivation is slow, unglamorous, and resistant to scale.

This is why technological progress consistently outpaces moral progress. The tools improve exponentially. The users improve incrementally—if at all.

Consider how often we announce the end of old problems. The end of scarcity. The end of inequality. The end of conflict. The end of loneliness.

And then watch how quickly those problems reappear in updated forms.

Scarcity becomes psychological.
Inequality becomes digital.

Conflict becomes ideological.
Loneliness becomes connected.

Progress doesn't remove the problems—it relocates them.

This is why each generation ends up asking the same questions with new vocabulary. Why do we feel overwhelmed despite convenience? Why does abundance still produce anxiety?[2] Why do we feel watched, compared, measured, and judged—even when life is objectively easier than it was for those before us?

The answer is uncomfortable because it limits how exceptional we get to feel.

We are not the first to live with abundance and confusion at the same time. We are not the first to mistake novelty for improvement. We are not the first to believe that better tools would finally fix what better tools have never fixed.

Progress keeps repeating itself because human nature keeps showing up unchanged at its centre.

That doesn't make progress meaningless. It makes it incomplete.

Progress is real. Medical advances extend life. Infrastructure reduces suffering. Education expands opportunity. Communication technologies collapse distance. None of this is trivial. All of it matters within its proper domain.

The problem isn't progress itself. The problem is what we expect it to do for us.

We expect it to resolve the existential questions it was never designed to address. We expect external improvements to produce internal transformation. We expect accelerating capacity to generate some accelerating wisdom.

It doesn't.

Wisdom remains manual. Character remains slow. Maturity still requires failure, discomfort, and time—none of which are scalable. You can distribute technology to billions overnight. You cannot distribute self-awareness, restraint, or depth of soul at any speed.

This gap—between what we can build and what we can become—is where the disappointment lives.

Once you accept this, something shifts. You stop waiting for the next breakthrough to rescue you from the human condition. You stop expecting systems to produce what only maturity can sustain. You stop confusing momentum with direction.

You begin to treat progress more soberly—grateful for its benefits, alert to its limits.

This is where many people feel a twinge of disappointment. If progress can't save us, what will?

But again, that question rushes ahead too far.

The quieter, more useful insight comes first: progress is a tool, not a destination. It improves conditions. It does not resolve meaning. It extends possibilities. It does not tell us which ones are worth choosing.

When you expect progress to do what it cannot, you end up disillusioned. When you expect it to do only what it can, you end up freer.

You can enjoy the conveniences without demanding they complete you. You can celebrate innovations without pretending they've exempted you from human limitation. You can participate in advancement without needing it to vindicate your existence or your era.

History stops feeling like a failure to advance and starts looking like a mirror we keep glancing away from.

The same struggles return because they're rooted in something progress doesn't touch: the gap between what we want and what satisfies, between what we build and what we become, between our capacity to act and our capacity to choose wisely.

No amount of innovation closes that gap. It only makes the gap more visible.

Under the sun, there really is nothing new—not because nothing changes, but because the core struggles keep returning, asking the same questions in different accents.

We keep discovering that power doesn't ennoble. That wealth doesn't satisfy. That fame doesn't fulfil. That convenience doesn't liberate. That connection doesn't cure loneliness. That information doesn't guarantee wisdom.

Each generation learns this again, as if for the first time.

And each generation initially believes that *this time* will be different—that we've finally accumulated enough knowledge, enough technology, enough awareness to transcend the pattern.

We haven't.

We won't.

Not because we're failures, but because the pattern isn't a bug. It's a feature of the human condition under the sun. Progress changes what we can do. It doesn't change what we are.

The sooner we recognise the pattern, the less surprised we are when it repeats.

And the less tempted we are to believe that the next version will finally exempt us from being human.

Chapter 3: Why Chasing Pleasure Never Works for Long

Anthony Bourdain spent his career professionally pursuing pleasure. He travelled to every corner of the world. He ate foods most people will never taste. He drank rare wines. He met fascinating people. He turned curiosity into a lucrative art form.

By conventional measures, he had optimised his life for experience, for sensation, for precisely the kind of pleasure people fantasise about when they're stuck in traffic or sitting in cubicles.

And yet, near the end of his life, he often spoke of emptiness. Not in the dramatic way people describe depression—though that was present too—but in a quieter, more persistent way. The pleasure still worked in the moment. The meals were still excellent. The travel was still stimulating. But the satisfaction had become increasingly thin, increasingly temporary.

The returns were diminishing faster than the appetite for them.

He wasn't alone in this. He was just more honest about it than most.

There is a moment, usually brief, when pleasure delivers precisely what it promises.

The holiday where you forget your email exists.
The meal that silences conversation.
The purchase that feels oddly justified.
The relationship that makes ordinary life seem suddenly brighter.

For a while, it works.

Then—almost without announcing itself—the feeling fades. Not dramatically. Not cruelly. Just quietly. What once felt intense becomes familiar. What once felt indulgent becomes expected. What once felt satisfying begins to ask for repetition.

More often.
More intensely.
With higher stakes.

This is where most people make their mistake.

They assume the problem is moderation, timing, or access. They think pleasure failed because it wasn't pursued carefully enough, strategically enough, or boldly enough. So, they adjust the method rather than questioning the pursuit.

The chase continues.

Modern life makes this easy. Pleasure has never been more available, more customizable, or more socially acceptable. Entertainment is endless. Food is engineered for maximum palatability. Desire is studied, predicted, and nudged through algorithms that know what you want before you consciously register wanting it.

Streaming platforms eliminate the friction of choice paralysis by auto-playing the next episode. Food scientists design snacks to hit the "bliss point"—the precise ratio of salt, sugar, and fat that keeps you reaching for more. Dating apps gamify connection. Shopping apps gamify acquisition. Even productivity is gamified, turning work into a series of dopamine-triggering completions.

The barriers that once slowed gratification have largely disappeared.

And yet satisfaction remains stubbornly short-lived.

Neuroscience has a term for this pattern: dopamine adaptation. Dopamine is not the chemical of pleasure itself, but of anticipation. It motivates pursuit. It spikes before reward, not during it. The brain is designed to normalise repeated stimuli quickly, reducing their impact over time.

In simple terms, pleasure works best the first few times.[1]

This isn't a flaw. It's a survival feature. Without adaptation, humans would become fixated on a single source of pleasure and stop exploring. But when pleasure becomes a primary strategy for meaning or relief, the system turns against us. What once soothed begins to demand escalation. What once satisfied begins to feel thin.

So, the cycle intensifies.

This is why abundance often produces restlessness rather than contentment, why boredom thrives in environments designed to eliminate it. Why do people surrounded by stimulation still complain of emptiness?

Pleasure was never meant to carry the weight we place on it.

History has observed this long before science measured it. Cultures that equated pleasure with the good life tended to produce refinement—and then fatigue.

Consider the late Roman Empire. The aristocracy had perfected leisure. They had elaborate baths, theatrical performances, gladiatorial spectacles, and imported delicacies from across the known world. They engineered pleasure with the same ingenuity they brought to aqueducts and roads.

And yet, the literature of the period is filled with complaints of ennui. Seneca wrote about the restlessness of men who had everything and felt nothing. They travelled compulsively, not because travel delighted them, but because staying still had become unbearable. They threw more elaborate parties, not because parties satisfied them, but because ordinary evenings felt like deprivation.

Excess did not destroy desire. It dulled it. Sensation became background noise.

What's striking is how consistently this pattern repeats across time, class, and technology. The form of pleasure changes, but the effect does not. Whether through food, sex, entertainment, substances, or status, the result is familiar: diminishing returns followed by quiet dissatisfaction.

This doesn't mean pleasure is bad.

It means pleasure is limited.

Modern psychology reinforces this distinction. Research by Daniel Kahneman demonstrates that pleasure contributes to happiness in short bursts, but beyond a certain threshold, it loses its influence on long-term well-being.[2] Meaning, purpose, and relational depth—things far less stimulating—prove far more durable predictors of sustained satisfaction.

Yet pleasure remains more attractive because it is immediate, measurable, and easy to sell.

So, we build lives around it.

We curate experiences.
We optimise comfort.
We avoid discomfort wherever possible.

And then we wonder why resilience feels rare.

Pleasure temporarily numbs pain, but it also numbs contrast. When everything is designed to feel good, the capacity to enjoy anything deeply begins to erode. **Joy, unlike pleasure, depends on contrast.** It requires patience, limitation, and often restraint.

A meal tastes better when you've been hungry. Rest feels sweeter when you've been tired. Relief is only relief after tension. Entertainment only delights when boredom has created space for it.

But when pleasure is constant, contrast disappears. The baseline rises. And with it, the threshold for what registers as satisfying.

This is why people who chase pleasure hardest often struggle most with stillness. Silence feels uncomfortable. Boredom feels threatening.

Ordinary life feels inadequate. The baseline has been artificially raised, and now everything below that baseline feels like deprivation.

Sociologists describe this as the hedonic treadmill: no matter how much pleasure increases, satisfaction remains roughly the same because expectations rise in parallel.[3] **The scenery changes. The speed increases. The destination does not.**

What's rarely acknowledged is the emotional cost of this treadmill. When pleasure becomes central, suffering feels like a failure. Discomfort feels unacceptable. Pain feels unnecessary.

But pain is unavoidable.

So instead of integrating it, we distract from it. **We entertain ourselves out of awareness.** We scroll, snack, binge, buy, and buffer our way through life—not realising that in doing so, we also buffer our capacity for joy.

We protect ourselves from feeling bad, but in the process, we numb our capacity to feel good.

This is where the experiment quietly collapses.

Pleasure can enhance life.
It cannot sustain it.

When pleasure becomes the answer to existential questions, it inevitably disappoints. Not because it lied—but because it was never designed to answer them.

What will make me happy?
What will make life feel meaningful?
What will finally satisfy this restlessness?

Pleasure can't answer those. It can only distract them temporarily.

The problem isn't that people seek pleasure. The problem is that we've elevated pleasure from a feature of life to the *purpose* of life. We've turned it into a metric for success, a measure of whether we're living well, a litmus test for whether life is working.

When it fails to deliver—when the high fades, when the vacation ends, when the purchase loses its sheen—we assume we did it wrong. We chose the wrong pleasure. We didn't optimise properly. We need to try harder.

We rarely consider that the expectation itself is the problem.

Once this becomes clear, the relationship with pleasure changes. It loses its authority. It becomes a guest rather than a ruler. Enjoyed when present. Released when absent.

This doesn't mean rejecting pleasure. It means right-sizing it.

You can enjoy a good meal without needing it to validate your life. You can take a vacation without expecting it to heal your soul. You can appreciate comfort without demanding it be constant. You can indulge occasionally without making it your identity.

Pleasure returns to its proper place: a gift, not a goal.

When you stop asking pleasure to do what it cannot do, something unexpected happens. Pleasure becomes lighter. Less demanding. Less tyrannical. And paradoxically, more enjoyable.

Because you're no longer interrogating it. You're no longer measuring it against impossible standards. You're no longer disappointed when it fades, because you never expected it to last.

Under the sun, chasing pleasure always ends the same way—not with ruin, but with restlessness. The appetite grows. The satisfaction shrinks. The soul remains unconvinced.

The Teacher in Ecclesiastes tried this experiment exhaustively. Wine, music, gardens, servants, wealth, sexual pleasure—he pursued it all systematically, leaving nothing untried. And his conclusion was stark: "Behold, all was vanity and a striving after wind."

Not because the pleasures weren't real. They were. But because they couldn't bear the weight of the meaning he tried to place on them.

Two thousand years later, the experiment repeats. Different forms, same outcome. The modern version has better marketing.

But when pleasure is received rather than pursued, something shifts. It becomes lighter. Less demanding. Less central.

And strangely, more enjoyable.

Chapter 4: The Lie of Productivity as Identity

When Margaret Obi retired at 62, she had all the markers of a successful career behind her. Three decades in corporate strategy. Multiple promotions. Solid pension. Good health. Her colleagues threw her a party. Her boss gave a speech about her contributions. Everyone said she'd earned it.

Six months later, she was in therapy, trying to explain a feeling she couldn't quite name.

It wasn't that she missed the work itself—the meetings, the deadlines, the office politics. She didn't. What unsettled her was something stranger: she no longer knew how to introduce herself. When people asked what she did, the answer felt like an amputation. "I'm retired" sounded like "I'm no one."

Her calendar, once colour-coded and packed, now stared back at her with blank spaces that felt accusatory. She found herself checking email obsessively, even though there were none left. She cleaned the house repeatedly. She volunteered aggressively. Anything to avoid the quiet question underneath it all:

If I'm not producing, who am I?

She hadn't chosen to fuse her identity with her output. It had happened gradually, through decades of performance reviews, promotions that affirmed her worth, and a culture that consistently equated busyness with importance.

When the work ended, the scaffolding collapsed.

One of the most revealing questions you can ask someone today is not what they believe, but how busy they are.

Busyness has become a form of self-description.
An explanation.
A quiet justification.

Ask how someone is doing, and the answer often comes preloaded: busy, swamped, flat out, non-stop. It's said with a hint of complaint and a hint of pride, as though exhaustion itself were evidence of value.

This is new.

Work has always been necessary. Labour has always shaped life. But only recently has productivity been asked to explain who we are.

We don't just work anymore.
We perform usefulness.

Modern work culture rarely states this outright, but it enforces it subtly and relentlessly: your worth is visible, measurable, and ideally increasing. Output is tracked. Availability is assumed. Idleness is suspicious.

Rest, when permitted, must be justified.

So, people adapt. They optimise themselves. They brand their effort. They turn calendars into proof of existence. They learn to feel uneasy when nothing is scheduled, as though unscheduled time were a kind of moral failure.

The irony is that most people didn't choose this consciously. It emerged gradually, through incentives and systems that reward constant motion.

Email erased the boundary between work time and personal time. The expectation of immediate response transformed communication into an unending stream of micro-obligations. Smartphones collapsed the distinction between being at work and being available for work—suddenly, you were always both.

Metrics replaced judgment. When everything can be quantified—emails sent, tasks completed, hours logged, meetings attended—productivity becomes a score that can be compared, ranked, and optimised. Hustle became admirable, repackaged as ambition and drive. Stillness became inefficient, reframed as laziness or lack of commitment.

And slowly, productivity stopped being something we do and started becoming something we are.

Sociologist Richard Sennett documents this transformation precisely in *The Corrosion of Character.* In industrial economies, work once answered the question "What do you do?" In post-industrial economies, it increasingly answers *"Who are you?"* When identity attaches to output, the stakes change fundamentally. Work no longer ends when the task is finished; it ends when the person is finished.

That's when the trouble begins.

People who derive identity from productivity struggle most when productivity falters.[1] Illness feels like failure. Slowness feels like guilt. Ageing feels like irrelevance. Even leisure becomes performative—optimised, documented, and evaluated for usefulness.

This is why burnout today often arrives with confusion rather than anger. People don't say, "I hate my job." They say, "I don't know who I am without it."

The lie at the centre of this culture is simple but persuasive: that constant usefulness equals lasting significance.

It doesn't.

Usefulness is real, but it is temporary. Every role expires. Every skill ages. Every system eventually replaces its own experts. Productivity can justify a season of life; it cannot justify a life.

History bears this out relentlessly. Entire professions rise, dominate, and vanish within a generation. Elevator operators. Switchboard operators. Travel agents. Video rental clerks. Jobs that once employed millions and seemed permanent evaporated as technology and culture shifted.

Skills once indispensable become obsolete. The typist, the telegraph operator, the stenographer—roles that required years of training and represented respectable careers—disappeared almost overnight. Workers once celebrated become invisible. The system does not mourn. It moves on.

And yet we continue to offer ourselves to it as though it were capable of remembering us.

Research by Christina Maslach demonstrates that while meaningful work contributes to well-being, over-identification with work correlates strongly with anxiety, depression, and emotional exhaustion.[2] The problem is not effort. It is fusion—when self-worth and output become indistinguishable.

When productivity becomes identity, rest feels dangerous. *If I stop, who am I? If I slow down, do I still matter? If I am not producing, am I wasting something irreplaceable?*

Time, after all, feels scarce.

So, we hurry.

We fill space.
We multitask.
We measure ourselves against people we cannot see and standards we did not choose.

Technology makes this worse by removing natural limits. Work follows us home, into bed, into weekends, into holidays. Notifications erase pauses. The day never quite closes. There is always one more message, one more task, one more small thing that could be done "quickly."

Except it never is.

This is not because employers are uniquely cruel or workers uniquely weak. It is because systems optimise for output rather than humanity. They reward availability, not wisdom. Speed, not depth. Visibility, not sustainability.

And we internalise those rewards.

Eventually, people begin to fear the very things that once gave life texture: boredom, silence, unstructured time. These moments threaten to expose the truth productivity has been masking—that usefulness alone cannot carry the weight of meaning.

This is why retirement so often unsettles people. Not because they dislike rest, but because rest strips away the scaffolding work that provides identity. Without tasks, titles, and schedules, a quieter question emerges: *Who am I now?*

That question cannot be answered with a to-do list.

Here is the part that few productivity systems acknowledge: **humans are not designed for constant output. We are seasonal creatures.**

Energy rises and falls. Attention fluctuates. Capacity changes with age, health, and circumstance. To deny this is not discipline; it is denial.

Older cultures understood this better than we do. Work was necessary, but it was bounded by daylight, by seasons, by sabbath rhythms, by communal limits. Those boundaries did not make people lazy. They made work survivable.

Agricultural societies worked in cycles. Intense labour during planting and harvest gave way to quieter winters. The rhythm wasn't optional—it was ecological. You couldn't force crops to grow faster by working longer hours. The land itself imposed limits, and those limits created rest.

Sabbath practices—whether Jewish, Christian, or secular variants—institutionalised rhythmic rest. One day in seven was set aside, not as a reward for productivity, but as an acknowledgement of human limitation. Rest wasn't earned through sufficient output. It was built into the structure of time itself.

Even the medieval European peasant, often portrayed as oppressed and overworked, had more structured rest than the modern knowledge worker. Saints' days, seasonal festivals, and guild regulations created a calendar punctuated by communal pause. Work was hard, but it was not endless.

The Industrial Revolution began to erode these boundaries. Factories needed constant operation. Shift work made time fungible. Electric light eliminated the natural limit of darkness. But even industrial work had clear start and end times. You clocked in, you clocked out. Work stayed at the factory.

What we have now is different. Digital work has no natural boundaries. Knowledge work never truly ends because there's always more that could be done, thought about, and improved. The project is never finished—only abandoned when the deadline arrives.

When productivity loses its limits, it also loses its meaning.

Work that never pauses cannot be savoured. An achievement that immediately demands the next achievement cannot satisfy. Progress that never rests cannot be appreciated. The rhythm collapses into monotony disguised as momentum.

The reckoning usually arrives quietly. A health scare. A breakdown. A sense of numbness. A realisation that years have passed in motion but not in presence. People wake up one day tired in a way sleep doesn't fix.

This is not a call to abandon work.
It is a call to demote it.

Work is a tool.
It is not a mirror.

Once productivity is returned to its proper place, something surprising happens. People often become better workers. More focused. More creative. Less frantic. Freed from proving their worth, they can give their effort without giving themselves away.

Rest becomes legitimate.
Limits become sane.
Silence becomes tolerable.

And identity—slowly—detaches from output.

You can work hard without believing your worth is being tested. You can contribute meaningfully without that contribution defining you. You can retire, or get sick, or slow down, without experiencing it as existential erasure.

Work becomes what it always should have been: one season among many, one activity among others, meaningful but not ultimate.

Under the sun, work has its place. It feeds, builds, and sustains. But when it is asked to define who we are, it eventually breaks us.

There is a time for planting and a time for harvest. A time for building and a time for resting. A time for striving and a time for stillness. The rhythm is not weakness—it is wisdom. The limits are not failures—they are features.

Productivity was never meant to tell you who you are.

Once you stop asking it to, work can finally become what it always should have been: meaningful, limited, and human-sized.

Chapter 5: Why Fairness Is Not Guaranteed

Cheryl Badmus had been a quality control manager at a medical device manufacturer for fourteen years. When she discovered that a supplier was falsifying safety test data on components used in cardiac implants, she reported it through the proper channels. Company policy, she was told, required her to escalate concerns to her supervisor first.

She did.

Her supervisor told her to document it and wait. The documentation sat in a file for three months while the components continued to be used. When she escalated again—this time to the compliance department—the company launched an investigation. Not into the supplier. Into her.

Within six months, her performance reviews mysteriously declined. Projects she'd successfully managed for years were suddenly cited as examples of poor judgment. Her position was "restructured," and she was offered a demotion or severance.

She took severance and filed a whistleblower complaint.

The supplier eventually paid a fine and kept their contract. The supervisor who ignored her warning was promoted. Cheryl struggled to find work in her industry. Background checks led to quiet conversations with her former employer. Opportunities evaporated.

Years later, she still can't quite explain the feeling. Not anger, exactly—though that was there too. It was something more profound: the disorienting realisation that doing the right thing had been actively punished while cutting corners had been rewarded. The world wasn't supposed to work that way.

But it did.

One of the first things children learn—and one of the hardest things adults unlearn—is the idea that life is supposed to be fair.

We don't usually say it out loud, but we live as though it were true. We expect effort to be rewarded, honesty to be recognised, and kindness to be returned. When those expectations are met, we call it justice. When they aren't, we feel cheated.

The strength of this belief lies in how reasonable it sounds.

Why shouldn't good behaviour lead to good outcomes?
Why shouldn't integrity protect us?
Why shouldn't hard work eventually pay off?

These assumptions feel moral. They feel civilised. They feel necessary.

And yet, lived experience keeps interrupting them.

People cut corners and advance.
People act honourably and fall behind.
Those who exploit systems often prosper within them.
Those who refuse are told to be patient.

This is not new. It's just newly documented.

Modern societies like to believe they have outgrown injustice—that with enough transparency, regulation, and education, fairness will eventually become automatic. But inequality persists not only economically but also relationally, politically, and morally.

The rules exist.
The outcomes don't always follow.

This gap between expectation and reality is where resentment takes root.

Resentment is not anger at wrongdoing. It is anger at unrewarded virtue. It grows when people do what they believe is right and discover that rightness offers no protection. Over time, resentment corrodes trust—not only in systems but also in the idea that behaviour matters at all.

The progression is subtle but predictable. First comes confusion: *Why didn't my honesty pay off?* Then frustration: *Others cheat and prosper.* Then bitterness: *The game is rigged.* And finally, cynicism: *Maybe virtue is just naiveté.*

Each stage feels like waking up. Each stage also represents a loss—not of goodness exactly, but of the belief that goodness will be recognised or rewarded.

This is where envy enters quietly.

Envy is not simply wanting what someone else has. It is the discomfort of seeing someone receive what we believe should have been ours. It thrives in environments where comparison is constant and moral accounting is assumed. If life is fair, then success must be deserved. And if success is deserved, then someone else's gain must explain our loss.

As economist Robert Frank documents in *Success and Luck*, societies with strong meritocratic ideals often experience more resentment, not less. When outcomes are framed as purely earned, inequality feels personal. Failure becomes a verdict on character rather than circumstance.[1] Success becomes proof of virtue rather than luck.

Fairness, ironically, becomes a weapon.

It allows the successful to feel morally superior. It allows the struggling to feel morally inadequate. It transforms structural inequalities into personal judgments. And it teaches everyone to constantly audit their lives against others, measuring virtue by outcomes.

This is why injustice unsettles us more than hardship. Suffering we can endure. Unfairness offends our sense of order. We can accept pain more easily than arbitrariness.

So, we construct explanations.

We tell ourselves that those who succeed must be smarter, better connected, less ethical, or secretly miserable. We tell ourselves that those who suffer must have made poor choices, lacked discipline, or somehow deserve it. These stories help restore a sense of balance—even when they distort reality.

But reality resists simplification.

History offers endless evidence that moral accounting does not function like a ledger. Virtue does not guarantee prosperity. Corruption does not always lead to collapse. Power protects itself. Systems reward what they measure, not what they praise.

Consider Ignaz Semmelweis, the 19th-century physician who discovered that handwashing dramatically reduced maternal mortality in hospitals. His data was precise. His logic was sound. His recommendations were cost-effective and straightforward.

He was mocked, ostracised, and eventually fired. His colleagues found his findings insulting—the implication that *they* were causing deaths through poor hygiene was unacceptable. Semmelweis spent his final years in a mental asylum, where he died of an infection at 47.

Within a decade of his death, germ theory vindicated him completely. But vindication didn't save him. His integrity didn't protect him. His correctness didn't matter when power decided otherwise.

The pattern repeats endlessly. Whistleblowers are punished while fraudsters are promoted. Truth-tellers are marginalised while liars prosper. Reformers are silenced while exploiters thrive—at least for a while, and often for long enough that it doesn't matter.

And yet we keep expecting life to behave like a courtroom.

This expectation is deeply human. It gives structure to chaos. It allows us to believe that outcomes are intelligible, that suffering has a reason, and that the world is ultimately manageable.

But when fairness becomes a guarantee rather than a hope, it turns cruel.

Because then every injustice feels like betrayal. Every loss feels personal. Every delay feels like a punishment. And eventually, bitterness begins to masquerade as insight.

This is where many people quietly lose their moral footing. When fairness fails, they conclude that morality itself must be naïve. *If integrity doesn't protect me, why bother? If honesty doesn't advance me, why persist? If kindness isn't returned, why offer it?*

The danger is subtle. People don't abandon virtue all at once. They adjust it. They rationalise small compromises. They justify exceptions. They learn to survive in a system they no longer trust.

A manager who once valued transparency starts protecting themselves first. A worker who prides themselves on honesty learns strategic silence. A professional who believed in merit begins to work the political angles. None of them set out to become cynical. They adapted.

The irony is that injustice not only harms its victims but also harms society as a whole. It reshapes its observers. It teaches people what not to expect, and over time, what not to value.

Children watch adults cut corners and succeed. They learn. Employees watch ethical colleagues get passed over. They learn. Citizens watch corrupt officials go unpunished. They learn.

The lesson isn't written in any handbook, but it gets transmitted efficiently: virtue is optional, outcomes matter, and the game is rigged in favour of those willing to exploit it.

Research by Richard Wilkinson and Kate Pickett demonstrates that persistent unfairness erodes social trust, well-being, and cohesion far more powerfully than absolute poverty.[2] When people believe the game is rigged, cooperation declines. Cynicism rises. Trust collapses.

Not because people become worse—but because they adapt.

This is where the limits of moral accounting become clear. **Life does not distribute outcomes according to virtue. It distributes them according to power, timing, chance, and structure.** Moral behaviour still matters—but not because it guarantees reward.

That distinction is crucial.

When goodness is practised as a transaction—I'll be honest, *so I'll be rewarded*—it will eventually disappoint. When it is practised as a posture—I'll be honest, *because that's who I choose to be*—it can survive disappointment.

The most disorienting realisation for many people is this: **fairness is not promised, but responsibility remains.** We are still accountable for who we become, even when outcomes mock our efforts.

This feels unjust—because it is.

But it is also clarifying.

Once we stop expecting the world to keep score correctly, we are forced to decide what kind of people we want to be without guarantees. Integrity becomes less strategic and more honest. Kindness becomes less conditional. Envy loses some of its grip because comparison no longer serves as proof of worth.

You can act with integrity even when it costs you, because your integrity isn't contingent on reward. You can refuse to exploit others even when exploitation is profitable, because your character isn't for sale. You can offer kindness even when it's not returned, because your kindness isn't a transaction.

This doesn't resolve injustice.
It doesn't excuse it.
It doesn't romanticise suffering.

It simply removes the illusion that fairness is automatic.

Under the sun, injustice exists. It always has. It always will. The world does not reliably reward the good or punish the wicked. Expecting it to do so is understandable—but costly.

The Teacher in Ecclesiastes observed this thousands of years ago and found it profoundly troubling: "There are righteous people to whom it happens according to the deeds of the wicked, and there are wicked people to whom it happens according to the deeds of the righteous."

The observation hasn't aged. The problem hasn't been solved.

What *has* changed is our capacity to document injustice more thoroughly, to measure inequality more precisely, to see clearly just how arbitrary outcomes can be. We have more data. We don't have more fairness.

Once that expectation is released, something steadier can take its place: not optimism, not resignation, but realism. A realism that acknowledges the limits of moral accounting while still choosing to live with intention.

Realism sees injustice clearly without being paralysed by it. It recognises that systems are broken without concluding that virtue is pointless. It accepts that outcomes are often arbitrary without abandoning responsibility for character.

Fairness may not be guaranteed.

Chapter 6: Why Money Can't Make You Feel Secure

The email arrives late at night.

It's short. Polite. Vague.
"We'll need to revisit projections."
"Let's regroup next quarter."

Nothing catastrophic is said.
Nothing reassuring either.

And suddenly, sleep feels optional.

The bank balance hasn't changed.
The house is still there.
The income is still coming—for now.

But something essential has shifted.

Security, it turns out, was never sitting in the numbers. It was based on the assumption that the numbers had permanent meaning.

David McPherson sold his software company in 2019 for $11 million. After taxes, legal fees, and settling debts, he walked away with roughly $7 million—more money than he'd ever imagined having, certainly more than he needed for a comfortable life.

He expected to feel relief. Security. The freedom that comes from knowing you're set.

Instead, he felt more anxious than ever.

The money sat in various accounts and investments, but it no longer felt like *his* exactly. It felt like something he was *managing*—a portfolio that could shrink, a nest egg that could crack, a fortune that could evaporate if he made the wrong choices. He obsessively checked market performance. He second-guessed his financial advisor. He lay awake calculating: Was $7 million enough if he lived to 95? What if healthcare costs exploded? What if inflation accelerated? What if the market crashed like in 2008?

Before the sale, his concerns had been simpler: Can we pay the mortgage? Can we afford a vacation? Now his concerns were more complex but somehow more consuming: How do I protect this? How do I grow it safely? How do I know when enough is enough?

The irony wasn't lost on him. He'd worked for years, believing that financial security would bring peace. Instead, having money to lose felt more stressful than not having enough in the first place.

The fear isn't poverty—it's reversal.

Money has a strange power. Not because it guarantees safety—but because it creates the illusion that safety can be guaranteed.

For a while, it works.

Money removes immediate threats. It smooths the inconvenience. It buys time, choice, and insulation from certain kinds of chaos. Compared to not having it, having it feels like relief.

So, we draw a conclusion we rarely question: more money will mean more security.

But watch closely what actually happens.

As income rises, so do obligations.
As assets grow, so do anxieties.
As lifestyles expand, so does what can be lost.

What money removes at one level, it reintroduces at another.

When you have little, you worry about making rent. When you have more, you worry about property taxes, maintenance, insurance premiums, and whether the neighbourhood is declining. The worry doesn't disappear—it upgrades.

With a modest income, you manage one bank account. With significant wealth, you manage diversified portfolios, tax strategies, estate planning, and trust structures. The financial life becomes more complex, not simpler. And complexity breeds new forms of anxiety: Am I optimised correctly? Did I miss something? Is my advisor competent?

Children's education becomes not just a concern but a competitive anxiety. Healthcare becomes not just access but optimisation. Retirement becomes not just a matter of feasibility but of lifestyle maintenance. Each worry morphs from *Can I afford this?* to *Can I afford to maintain this standard indefinitely?*

This is why people who appear financially "set" often live with a low-grade tension they struggle to name. **The concern shifts from *Can I survive?* to *Can I maintain?***

Research by Daniel Kahneman and Angus Deaton documents this pattern precisely. Once basic needs are met, money's ability to reduce anxiety drops sharply. Beyond approximately $75,000 in annual income (in 2010 dollars), additional money does little to improve day-to-day emotional well-being.[1] Life evaluation—how people think about their lives—continues to improve with income. But moment-to-moment happiness and anxiety levels plateau or even worsen as wealth increases.

In other words: **money solves problems—then replaces them.**

This isn't because people are ungrateful.
It's because security is not the same as comfort.

Money excels at comfort.
Security lives somewhere else.

Security has more to do with predictability, trust, and control—three things money appears to offer, but cannot reliably deliver.

Markets fluctuate.
Jobs disappear.
Currencies weaken.
Health changes.
Relationships fracture.

Money can cushion the fall, but it cannot stop the ground from shifting.

The 2008 financial crisis revealed this starkly. People who'd spent decades building retirement accounts watched them halve in value almost overnight. Diversification strategies intended to protect against volatility failed because *everything* declined at the same time. The ground shifted beneath the entire system.

Homeowners who'd believed real estate was the ultimate secure investment discovered that houses could lose 40% of their value. Executives at stable corporations discovered their pensions weren't as guaranteed as they'd assumed. Retirees discovered that "safe" bonds could turn toxic.

The wealthy weren't immune—in some ways, they suffered more psychological shock. They'd done everything "right": saved aggressively, appropriately diversified, and hired advisors. And still, the security they thought they'd purchased evaporated.

This is why financial anxiety often increases in objectively wealthier societies. The stakes are higher. The losses are larger. The comparisons are relentless. When everyone around you seems to be "doing well," instability feels personal rather than structural.

Richard Wilkinson and Kate Pickett identify this as status anxiety—the fear of falling behind in a hierarchy that never stops rearranging itself. Money becomes not just a resource, but a scoreboard.[2] And scoreboards, as we've already seen, never sleep.

As Robert Frank documents, relative income comparisons intensify insecurity even amid overall wealth growth. When your reference group shifts upward—when your neighbours upgrade, your colleagues earn more, your college classmates achieve visible success—what feels like "enough" constantly escalates. A $200,000 income feels secure until you're surrounded by people earning $400,000. Then it feels precarious.[3]

The treadmill has no endpoint because comparison has no ceiling.

So, people respond rationally—by trying to lock security down.

They diversify.
They ensure.
They hedge.
They save aggressively.

None of these is foolish. But they are often asked to do more than they can.

Because beneath the spreadsheets sits a more profound hope: **If I plan carefully enough, I can outrun uncertainty.**

That hope does not age well.

History has an inconvenient habit of intruding on financial confidence. Entire fortunes have evaporated through inflation, war, fraud, policy shifts, or plain miscalculation. What felt solid one decade becomes fragile the next.

During the Great Depression, investors who'd been wealthy on paper in 1928 were destitute by 1932. Banking systems collapsed. Savings disappeared. The wealthy jumped from buildings not because they'd become poor in absolute terms, but because they couldn't reconcile their identity with their losses.

Weimar Germany's hyperinflation turned life savings into worthlessness within months. A wheelbarrow of cash couldn't buy bread. People who'd worked their entire lives and saved prudently watched their security literally devalue to nothing.

More recently, Argentina's 2001 economic collapse trapped middle-class savings in frozen bank accounts. People who thought they were secure discovered overnight that their money wasn't actually accessible. The system itself had failed.

What's striking is not that wealth proves unstable—but that we continue to expect stability from it.

This expectation quietly reshapes character. It trains people to equate security with accumulation, caution with wisdom, and risk with irresponsibility. Over time, **fear begins to masquerade as prudence.**

People stop asking, *"What is enough?"*
They start asking, "*What if it's not enough?*"

And that question has no ceiling.

Every milestone reveals another horizon. First, it's: *If I just had $100,000 saved, I'd feel secure.* Then it's $500,000. Then $1 million. Then $2 million. The number keeps rising because the underlying fear never gets addressed—it just finds new thresholds to attach itself to.

The paradox is this: **the more money is demanded in return for existential security, the more insecure its holders often feel.** Because now their peace depends on forces they cannot control—markets, systems, decisions made far away by people they will never meet.

Money was never meant to carry that weight.

This doesn't mean money is unimportant. It matters deeply. Lack of it creates real suffering. Pretending otherwise is dishonest.

But confusing money with security creates a different kind of suffering—quieter, more chronic, and more complex, to name a few.

Absolute security, such as it exists, comes from sources money can support but not supply.

Relationships that hold under pressure. Not transactional connections, but bonds tested by hardship and still intact. People who show up when nothing can be gained from showing up. Communities that function as mutual aid networks, not just social networks.

Skills that transfer across contexts. Not credentials that age out, but capacities that remain valuable regardless of which systems are rising or falling. Resourcefulness. Adaptability. The ability to create value in changed circumstances.

Communities that share risk. Not insurance products, but actual people who redistribute the burden when someone falls. The neighbour who brings meals. The friend who offers temporary housing. The network that catches you when systems don't.

And most importantly: **an inner posture that accepts uncertainty rather than trying to purchase immunity from it.**

That last one is the hardest.

Because it requires letting go of the fantasy that enough money will finally make life predictable.

It requires recognising that control was always partial, that prediction was always limited, that the ground was constantly shifting—and that no amount of wealth can change those facts.

This isn't a resignation. It's calibration. It's the difference between building a fortress (which will eventually be breached) and learning to walk steadily on unstable ground.

Under the sun, money won't provide existential security.

It can make life easier.
It can make life safer in practical ways.
It can make life more comfortable.

What it cannot do is remove fragility from being human.

Health fails regardless of bank balance. Relationships fracture regardless of net worth. Meaning remains elusive regardless of portfolio performance. Death arrives regardless of estate size.

Money can delay some of these. It can soften some of their impact. But it cannot exempt you from them.

Once that illusion dissolves, money becomes less tyrannical. It returns to its proper role—**a means, not a fortress.** Useful, but limited. Valuable, but unreliable as a source of peace.

And strangely, that's when people often handle it best.

Not because they have more of it—but because they've stopped asking it to protect them from the truth that no amount of it ever could.

Chapter 7: Why Intelligence Doesn't Save You

Intelligence has always been sold as a form of protection.

Learn enough, and you'll avoid mistakes.
Understand enough, and you'll see danger coming.
Think clearly, and life will make sense.

It's a comforting story—especially for those who have invested heavily in their minds.

Intelligence promises distance from chaos. It offers the hope that insight creates immunity. That if you can explain what's happening, you can somehow stay ahead of it.

For a while, this seems true.

Smart people often do better—academically, professionally, socially. They read the room. They spot patterns. They anticipate consequences. Compared to blind luck, intelligence looks like an upgrade.

But watch closely, and something odd appears.

Knowledgeable people still make disastrous decisions.
They still sabotage relationships.
They still misjudge timing.
They still chase what harms them.

And when things go wrong, they are often more confused than others, not less.

Robert McNamara was one of the brightest minds of his generation. Harvard Business School graduate. President of Ford Motor Company at 44. Secretary of Defence under Kennedy and Johnson. He brought systems analysis, statistical modelling, and rational decision-making frameworks to the Pentagon.

He could see patterns in data that others missed. He could process complexity that overwhelmed his peers. He understood strategic theory, game theory, and organisational behaviour at a level few could match.

And he led the United States deeper into Vietnam despite understanding—intellectually—that the war was unwinnable.

His intelligence didn't fail him. His analysis was often correct. He saw the problems. He named the risks. He predicted outcomes with disturbing accuracy in internal memos that remained classified for decades.

But he couldn't stop it.

Years later, in *The Fog of War*, McNamara reflected on the paradox: "We were wrong, terribly wrong. We owed it to future generations to explain why." But the explanation revealed something uncomfortable—his intelligence had illuminated the problem without providing control over it. He understood what was happening. He couldn't change course.

Intelligence, it turned out, was not the same as power.

This isn't anecdotal. Research by Keith Stanovich demonstrates that intelligence correlates weakly with real-world decision quality, especially under emotional pressure. Being smart improves analysis, not self-mastery. It sharpens reasoning, not restraint.[1]

In fact, **intelligence introduces its own vulnerabilities.**

The first is overconfidence. When people are used to being right in controlled environments—school, tests, professional domains with clear feedback—they begin to trust their judgments too much, especially in domains where feedback is slow, ambiguous, or distorted.

Smart people excel at pattern recognition. The problem is that they also excel at seeing patterns that aren't there, or at imposing order on randomness. They construct elegant explanations after the fact, which makes them less likely to notice errors in the moment. Intelligence becomes self-validating: *I understand this; therefore, my judgment is sound.*

The correlation between intelligence and overconfidence is well-documented. More intelligent people are more likely to believe they're correct even when they're wrong, because they can generate more sophisticated justifications for their positions.

The second vulnerability is rationalisation. Intelligence gives us better tools for justifying what we already want to do. We don't abandon poor decisions—we defend them more elegantly. The mind becomes an accomplice rather than a guard.

A less intelligent person might say, "I want this." A knowledgeable person constructs an elaborate framework to prove that wanting this is actually rational, strategic, and even morally justified. The intelligence serves the desire, not the truth.

This is why intelligent people often make worse decisions in personal relationships. They can rationalise red flags into green lights. They can explain away inconsistencies. They can build entire philosophies around why their dysfunctional choice is actually sophisticated.

The third vulnerability is the illusion of control. Understanding how things work can quietly morph into the belief that they will therefore work *for us.* That belief does not survive contact with chance.

When you understand probability, you might believe you can beat the odds. When you understand psychology, you might believe you can manipulate others reliably. When you understand markets, you might believe you can time them. Intelligence creates the illusion that the world is more predictable than it is.

History is full of brilliant individuals undone by forces they understood perfectly in theory.

Consider Long-Term Capital Management, the hedge fund founded in 1994 by financial luminaries including Myron Scholes and Robert

Merton, both Nobel Prize winners in economics. Their team included some of the most sophisticated quantitative minds in finance. They built mathematical models of unprecedented elegance to predict market behaviour and exploit tiny price inefficiencies.

The models worked brilliantly for years. The intelligence was real. The understanding was deep. They weren't gambling—they were applying rigorous statistical analysis to market dynamics.

Then in 1998, Russia defaulted on its debt. Markets behaved in ways the models deemed statistically impossible. Correlations that were supposed to be stable broke down simultaneously. The fund collapsed in a matter of weeks, losing $4.6 billion and nearly triggering a global financial crisis.

The Federal Reserve had to orchestrate a $3.6 billion bailout to prevent systemic collapse.

The intelligence didn't fail. The models weren't stupid. The understanding was genuine. What failed was the assumption that understanding creates control, that intelligence predicts the unpredictable, that being smart exempts you from chaos.

Because intelligence does not cancel uncertainty.

It negotiates with it.

Modern culture struggles to accept this because it places enormous faith in expertise. We educate, credential, analyse, model, and forecast. We assume that with enough data and intelligence, problems will yield to us.

Sometimes they do.

Often, they don't.

Economic crashes are rarely caused by ignorance. They are caused by intelligent people believing they have accounted for all variables. Political failures are not usually the result of stupidity, but of brilliant actors misjudging human behaviour. Personal disasters often come not from lack of insight, but from misplaced confidence in insight.

As political scientist Philip Tetlock's landmark study revealed, experts often perform no better than chance—and sometimes worse—in long-term forecasting despite high intelligence and deep expertise.[2] Specialists with PhDs, access to classified information, and decades of experience made predictions that were no more accurate than those of informed laypeople or simple algorithms.

High intelligence didn't translate to better prediction. It just created more elaborate explanations for why the predictions failed.

This creates a strange emotional burden for intelligent people.

When things go wrong, they feel personally indicted. *If I understood this, why didn't I avoid it? If I saw it coming, why couldn't I stop it?* Failure feels less like misfortune and more like self-betrayal.

So, they double down.

They analyse harder.
They replay conversations.
They search for the missing variable.

What they often discover—slowly and reluctantly—is that **life does not reward understanding with exemption.**

There is a reason why some of the most reflective people in history sounded weary rather than triumphant. **Knowledge expands awareness faster than it expands control.** The more you understand, the more clearly you see how much lies outside your reach.

You understand mortality but cannot escape it. You understand relationship dynamics but cannot prevent betrayal. You understand economic systems but cannot predict the next crisis. You understand your own psychology, but cannot always override it.

Intelligence illuminates the gap between how things are and how they ought to be. And that gap does not close with insight alone.

This is why intelligence often increases sorrow rather than removing it.[2] Not because ignorance is bliss, but because awareness widens the space between what you can see and what you can control. You become conscious of problems you cannot solve, patterns you cannot break, and tragedies you cannot prevent.

The fool doesn't worry about things they don't understand. The intelligent person lies awake thinking about things they understand perfectly but cannot change.

This is not an argument for ignorance. It is an observation about the cost of awareness. Intelligence is not free. The more you know, the more you carry. The clearer you see, the more you notice what's broken.

And that gap does not close with insight alone.

One of the most persistent myths of modern life is that better thinking will save us from human limits. But **limits do not disappear when named. They remain, fully intact, merely better described.**

Time still passes.
Bodies still weaken.
Chance still intervenes.
Other people still act unpredictably.

Intelligence does not override these realities. It observes them.

This is where many people feel disillusioned. *If being smart doesn't protect me, what was the point?*

The point was never protection.

Intelligence is a light, not a shield.

It helps you see.
It does not guarantee safety.

When intelligence is treated as a shield, it becomes brittle. People either grow arrogant—assuming they are immune—or anxious, believing they must think perfectly to survive. Both postures collapse under pressure.

When intelligence is treated as a light, it becomes humbler and more useful.

You use it to illuminate decisions without pretending to control outcomes.[3] You recognise risk without demanding certainty. You acknowledge what you don't know without treating that as personal failure. You make peace with the fact that understanding does not equal exemption.

This shift is subtle but profound.

You stop using intelligence to prove you deserve a good outcome.
You stop expecting insight to inoculate you against pain.
You stop confusing awareness with authority over life.

And something steadier takes its place.

You can be smart without needing your intelligence to save you. You can understand deeply without demanding that understanding protect you. You can see clearly without expecting clarity to change outcomes.

Intelligence becomes less about winning and more about witnessing. Less about control and more about honest observation. Less about exemption and more about participation.

Wisdom, as it turns out, is not intelligence with better answers. It is intelligence that has learned its limits.

Under the sun, being smart helps—but it does not save. It clarifies. It warns. It prepares.

What it does not do is guarantee escape.

The wise person and the fool both die. The intelligent person and the ignorant person both suffer loss. Understanding mortality doesn't prevent death. Seeing danger doesn't always allow you to avoid it. Predicting outcomes doesn't give you power over them.

Intelligence is valuable. But it is not a fortress.

Once that expectation is released, intelligence becomes less anxious, less defensive, and less self-important. It stops trying to win life and starts trying to understand it honestly.

That may not feel like triumph. But it is closer to the truth.

Chapter 8: Why Power Rewards the Wrong People

Most people don't want power.

They want what power seems to promise: security, autonomy, recognition, the ability to shape outcomes rather than endure them. Power looks like the antidote to vulnerability.

So, we tell ourselves a reassuring story: that power, over time, finds its way into responsible hands. Those systems improve. That competence rises. That merit eventually wins.

This story keeps us cooperative.

But history keeps interrupting it.

When the board of directors at Theranos needed a chairman, they appointed George Shultz—former Secretary of State, respected elder statesman, someone whose presence signalled credibility. His grandson, Tyler, worked at the company and raised concerns about fraudulent test results. Tyler had the data. He had the integrity. He went through the proper channels.

The board sided with Elizabeth Holmes.

Tyler was marginalised, then threatened with legal action. George Shultz, despite decades of diplomatic experience and stated commitment to truth, chose the institution over his grandson. Not because he was corrupt, but because the system applied pressure in ways that made institutional loyalty feel like wisdom.

Meanwhile, Holmes continued raising hundreds of millions in funding, despite mounting evidence that the technology didn't work. Investors, journalists, and board members wanted to believe. The confidence was there. The charisma was there. The willingness to dismiss sceptics as obstacles was there.

What wasn't there was the actual science.

Power didn't select the truth-teller. It selected the person most willing and able to perform, despite a lack of substance.

Again and again, power accumulates around people who are not especially wise, restrained, or morally serious. Sometimes they are competent. Often, they are not. What they almost always share is a willingness to pursue power for its own sake—and to tolerate costs others refuse.

This is not a glitch.
It is a selection effect.

Power does not reward the best people.
It rewards the most power-compatible ones.

The traits that help people acquire power are not the same as those that help them use it well. Ambition scales faster than conscience. Confidence outpaces caution. Ruthlessness travels lighter than restraint.

Someone who hesitates out of ethical concern loses ground to someone who doesn't hesitate at all. Someone who seeks consensus gets bypassed by someone who imposes decisions. Someone who admits uncertainty gets outmanoeuvred by someone who projects certainty even when they lack knowledge.

The system doesn't reward these behaviours because they're better. It rewards them because they're faster, more decisive, and less encumbered by second-guessing.

Research by psychologist Dacher Keltner documents this pattern with uncomfortable consistency. People who seek power are more likely to score higher in traits associated with dominance and lower in traits associated with empathy.[1] This does not make them villains. It makes them effective in competitive hierarchies.

And hierarchies select for effectiveness, not virtue.

This creates a tension most societies struggle to admit: **systems reward what they can measure and enforce, not what they admire.** Results matter more than intentions. Visibility outweighs integrity. Decisiveness beats deliberation.

So, power rises toward those least troubled by its costs.

This doesn't mean kind or ethical people never hold power. They do. But they often arrive reluctantly, temporarily, or at high personal cost. Many leave early. Others are pushed out. Some adapt in ways that surprise even themselves.

The system applies pressure.

Those who resist it are filtered out.
Those who comply rise.

Political sociologist Robert Michels described this as the "iron law of oligarchy" in his classic 1911 study of political parties. Even organisations founded on democratic principles inevitably drift toward concentrated power and institutional self-preservation.[2] The system selects leaders who prioritise organisational survival over original ideals—not because they're uniquely corrupt, but because survival becomes the primary criterion for selection.

From the outside, this looks like hypocrisy.
From the inside, it feels like a necessity.

The idealistic founder who refuses to compromise on mission gets replaced by a pragmatist who "understands how things work." The principled dissenter who slows decision-making gets sidelined in favour of someone who "gets things done." The careful thinker who raises concerns gets labelled an obstacle.

Each replacement feels justified in the moment. The cumulative effect is an organisation that no longer resembles its founding principles.

This is why corruption so often arrives gradually. Rarely does someone wake up intending to abuse power. More often, they make minor adjustments—justifiable compromises—in the name of efficiency, stability, or the greater good.

First, you bend a rule to meet a deadline. The deadline is absolute. The pressure is real. The compromise feels minor compared to the larger goal.

Then you overlook a colleague's ethical lapse because they're too valuable to lose right now. You'll address it later. Later never comes.

Then you authorise a decision you're uncomfortable with because the alternative is worse—or at least that's how it's framed. The framing becomes familiar. Your discomfort fades.

Each step feels reasonable. The cumulative effect does not.

Power has a way of teaching its own logic.

It rewards speed over reflection.
Control over cooperation.
Certainty over humility.

Those who question too much are labelled as obstacles. Those who hesitate are seen as weak. Those who slow things down are replaced by those who won't.

Power doesn't explicitly tell you to abandon your principles. It just makes abandoning them incrementally easier than maintaining them. And one day, you look up and realise you've become someone you wouldn't have recognised five years earlier.

This is why many intelligent, ethical people eventually opt out. Not because they lack conviction, but because they see the cost clearly. **Remaining clean often requires remaining marginal.**

And that realisation is deeply unsettling.

We want to believe the world is governed by moral gravity—that wrongdoing eventually collapses under its own weight, that justice has a built-in advantage. Sometimes this happens. Often it doesn't. Many abuses are never punished. Many opportunists retire comfortably.

Power protects itself well.

This is where envy enters again, sharper this time. Watching less capable people rise can corrode even principled minds. You did everything right. You worked harder. You maintained integrity. You refused shortcuts.

And you're still passed over while someone who cut corners, played politics, and compromised principles gets the promotion, the platform, the recognition.

The temptation is intense: *If the system rewards this behaviour, why am I refusing to engage in it? If integrity isn't actually rewarded, isn't maintaining it self-sabotage?*

The danger is not merely that power rewards the wrong people.

It's that prolonged exposure to this reality can deform the right ones.

The principled person starts making "strategic exceptions." The honest person learns when to stay silent. The ethical person begins distinguishing between "what I believe" and "what's practical." None of these feels like corruption in the moment. They feel like an adaptation.

And slowly, the person who entered the system as a corrective becomes another cog in its machinery.

This is how power doesn't just select certain personalities—it reshapes the ones it initially rejected. The idealist becomes the pragmatist. The reformer becomes the defender of the status quo. The critic becomes complicit.

Not through dramatic moral collapse, but through a thousand small accommodations that each seemed reasonable at the time.

Research demonstrates that power systematically alters perception. Those who hold it begin to overestimate their influence, underestimate risks, and discount dissent.[3] This isn't always arrogance. It's insulation. Feedback weakens as authority grows. Subordinates learn what not to say. Peers avoid confrontation. Critics are excluded from the room.

Power creates an echo chamber that validates itself. And within that chamber, compromise feels like wisdom, self-interest feels like strategy, and institutional preservation feels like responsibility.

So power doesn't just select certain personalities—it reshapes them.

This is why appeals to "good leadership" often disappoint. The problem is not that we fail to teach virtue. It's that the environments where power accumulates systematically undermine it.

Which leads to a tricky question most people avoid:

If power does not reliably reward goodness, why remain good?

For many, this is where cynicism hardens. They stop believing integrity matters. They conclude that outcomes justify methods. They trade principles for leverage. In doing so, they gain traction—and lose something more challenging to name.

Others retreat entirely, disengaging from influence out of disgust. They keep their hands clean, but surrender the field to those willing to get them dirty.

Neither response is satisfying.

The uncomfortable alternative is to accept a sobering truth: **power is morally indifferent. It amplifies what already exists. It does not refine it. It does not sanctify its holders. It does not distribute itself fairly.**

Once this is accepted, moral clarity can return—stripped of illusions.

You stop expecting power to validate virtue.
You stop confusing influence with worth.
You stop assuming success indicates righteousness.

And you begin to choose integrity without guarantees.

This is harder than idealism and lonelier than cynicism. It means acting responsibly even when it costs you advancement. It means resisting envy even when unfairness persists. It means refusing to become what the system rewards simply because it rewards it.

You can be passed over and remain principled. You can watch opportunists rise and refuse to imitate them. You can lose influence without losing character. You can exit power without bitterness or enter it without corruption—though both require constant vigilance.

The choice is never between effectiveness and integrity. The choice is whether to let power's distribution patterns dictate your moral posture.

Under the sun, power will continue to reward those best adapted to wield it—not those most deserving of it. That reality does not excuse wrongdoing. But it does clarify expectations.

The race is not to the swift, nor bread to the wise, nor riches to the intelligent, nor favour to those with knowledge—but time and chance happen to them all. Power is distributed according to its own logic, which is neither moral nor meritocratic.

The question then shifts from *Who gets power?* To Whom *do I become in its presence—or absence?*

Power will do what it has always done: concentrate around those most willing to pursue it, most able to tolerate its costs, most skilled at institutional manoeuvring.

What remains undecided is whether we allow it to define us.

Chapter 9: The Problem No One Escapes

Most of the ways we organise life are strategies for forgetting one thing.

We plan.
We ensure.
We optimise.
We distract ourselves.

Not because these are foolish, but because they help us keep death at a polite distance. We know it exists. We don't like to look at it directly.

Modern life is exceptionally good at this. Death has been professionalised, sanitised, delayed, and hidden behind institutions.[1] It happens in hospitals, not homes. Experts, not families, manage it. Bodies are removed quietly by professionals. Funerals are outsourced to industries. Grief is given timelines and stages, as though it were a project to be completed rather than a permanent alteration.

We encounter death as news, statistics, or tragedy—rarely as a personal certainty.

The language has changed, too. We talk about "passing," "losing someone," "end of life care"—gentle euphemisms that soften the stark fact. Medical systems speak of "treatment options" and "life extension" as though death were optional with sufficient intervention. Insurance companies calculate "life expectancy" as though it were a reliable metric rather than a guess.

Even the physical reality has been hidden. Previous generations washed and dressed their own dead, held wakes in living rooms, buried family in nearby cemeteries they visited regularly. Death was visible, present, integrated into the rhythm of life.

Now it happens elsewhere, handled by others, discussed in whispers.

And yet it remains the most democratic fact of existence.

No intelligence avoids it.
No wealth negotiates it away.
No power exempts itself.
No virtue postpones it indefinitely.

This is not pessimism.
It is arithmetic.

Paul Kalanithi was a neurosurgeon. Stanford graduate. Yale medical degree. On track for a prestigious academic career in neuroscience. At 36, he was diagnosed with stage IV lung cancer.

In his memoir *When Breath Becomes Air*, he described the strange recalibration that followed. Not the medical details—though those were harrowing—but the shift in what felt urgent.

Before diagnosis, his life had been structured around long-term milestones: finish residency, publish research, build a career, eventually start a family. The future was assumed to be spacious. Time felt expandable.

After diagnosis, that assumption evaporated.

Suddenly, questions that had felt abstract became visceral: *What makes life meaningful? What matters now, not eventually? What can I not leave undone?*

He didn't become a different person. He became himself with the pretence removed.

He finished his residency but stopped chasing the academic prestige he'd once pursued. He wrote instead. He had a daughter with his wife, knowing he might not see her grow up. He reconciled relationships. He stopped deferring what mattered.

Not because the cancer gave him new information about what was important. But because it stripped away the luxury of pretending, he had infinite time to figure it out later.

He died at 37, two years after diagnosis.

What he left behind wasn't optimism or defeat—it was clarity. The kind that only comes when later stops being guaranteed.

Every culture develops ways to soften this truth. Some mythologise it. Some spiritualize it. Some medicalise it. Western culture tends to postpone it—treating death as a technical problem to be solved rather than a condition to be lived with.

So, we talk about longevity instead of mortality.
Quality of life instead of finitude.
Risk factors instead of endings.

The language changes.
The reality does not.

What's striking is how much behaviour is shaped by what we refuse to acknowledge. Many ambitions, anxieties, and rivalries only make sense if time is assumed to be abundant. We behave as though life were expandable—as though there will always be another season to correct course, repair damage, or finally enjoy what we've been chasing.

We defer difficult conversations. We postpone reconciliations. We wait for the "right time" to pursue what matters. We treat the present as a rehearsal for a future that keeps receding.

But **time does not negotiate.**

Ernest Becker's foundational work, The Denial of Death, and subsequent Terror Management Theory research reveal that people oscillate between two responses to mortality: avoidance and overcompensation.[2] Some distract themselves endlessly—filling every moment with activity, entertainment, or work to avoid silence where awareness might creep in. Others attempt to build symbolic immortality through achievement, legacy, or recognition—hoping their work will outlive them, their name will be remembered, and their contribution will matter beyond their lifespan.

Both responses share the same assumption—that death must be neutralised to live well.

It cannot be.

Mortality is not a bug in the system.
It is the system.

Once this becomes clear, many cultural promises quietly collapse. The idea that life can be "figured out" with enough planning. The belief that success will eventually feel conclusive. The hope that meaning can be stockpiled for later enjoyment.

Later is not guaranteed.

This is why death is so disruptive. It does not simply end life; it exposes the fragility of the stories we tell ourselves about control, progress, and permanence.

And yet, paradoxically, it also clarifies.

People who have faced death closely—through illness, loss, or proximity—often describe the same strange shift.

Trivial concerns lose their grip. The argument that consumed you last week feels absurd. The promotion you were obsessing over feels less urgent. The grudge you've been nursing feels pointless. Not because these things don't matter at all, but because their importance suddenly reorders itself against a more apparent horizon.

Priorities recalibrate. Relationships that were being taken for granted suddenly feel precious. Time with people you love becomes non-negotiable. Experiences that were being deferred to "someday" are now. Work that felt mandatory becomes optional. Status competition that felt essential feels hollow.

Time feels heavier. An ordinary afternoon with your child becomes anything but ordinary. Conversations with an ageing parent stop being routine. A sunset stops being background. The present stops being something to rush through on the way to later.

Presence becomes sharper. You notice more. You're there more fully. Not because you've gained some mystical awareness, but because you've stopped living in the future tense.

Not because they have discovered new information, but because they have stopped pretending something they already knew.

Everyone knows intellectually that time is limited. But knowing it abstractly and feeling it viscerally are different. The first allows postponement. The second doesn't.

Research by psychologist Laura Carstensen confirms this pattern. Awareness of mortality tends to narrow focus toward what feels immediately meaningful: relationships, experiences, reconciliation, and contribution.[3] Status competition weakens. Long-term abstractions lose urgency. People stop caring what strangers think and start caring what they'll regret.

In other words, death does what no productivity system ever could—it tells the truth about what matters now.

This is deeply inconvenient.

It disrupts ambition.
It resists optimisation.
It mocks the idea that life is primarily about accumulation.

Which is why many people treat death as an interruption rather than a guide.

We schedule around it.
We euphemise it.
We keep it abstract.

But abstraction comes at a cost.

When mortality is ignored, life fills up with urgency but lacks gravity. Everything feels important because nothing is clearly limited. The calendar fills. The inbox overflows. The to-do list expands. But beneath the motion, there's a strange hollowness—busyness without depth, activity without direction.

You're always preparing for the next thing but never fully present for this thing.

This is why people often reach midlife surprised.

Not surprised they're ageing—that was always inevitable. Surprised by something else: that time has passed faster than expected. Those opportunities have closed quietly. Those specific paths are no longer available.

Not because of failure. Because **choice always narrows.**

The twenty-year-old has infinite possible futures. The forty-year-old has fewer. The sixty-year-old has fewer still, not as punishment, but as mathematics. Every choice forecloses others. Every year that passes removes options. Every relationship neglected becomes harder to repair. Every skill unpractised becomes harder to acquire.

The midlife crisis isn't about ageing. It's about belated realism—the shocked recognition that the time you thought you had isn't actually there anymore. That "someday" has quietly become "never." That the spaciousness you assumed was an illusion.

The shock is not ageing.
It is belated realism.

And the tragedy is that this realisation often comes too late to reshape life around it. The career has been built. The relationships have atrophied. The patterns have calcified. Awareness arrives, but leverage has diminished.

Under the sun, everyone eventually learns the same lesson—but not everyone learns it early enough to live differently because of it.

The unsettling truth is this: **death does not give life meaning—it reveals it.** It strips away the illusion that everything can be postponed. It exposes which values were borrowed and which were chosen. It shows what survives when time runs short.

This is why attempts to defeat death psychologically often backfire. When mortality is treated as the enemy, life becomes anxious and grasping. Every moment feels like it must be optimised, every opportunity maximised, every experience captured and preserved. The pressure becomes unbearable.

When death is acknowledged as a boundary, life becomes more intentional.

Boundaries do this.
They focus attention.
They force prioritisation.

A blank page is paralysing. A page with margins focuses the eye. An endless timeline creates diffusion. A limited timeline creates urgency—the good kind, where clarity replaces franticness.

Finitude is not the opposite of meaning.
It is the condition that makes meaning possible.

Without limits, nothing is urgent.
Without endings, nothing is precious.
Without mortality, life dissolves into endless postponement.

This is not comforting. But it is stabilising.

Once death is faced honestly, certain illusions lose their power.

The need to win every argument fades—what will it matter in fifty years? The pressure to maximise every opportunity weakens—you can't do everything, so what actually matters? The fear of missing out dissolves—missing out is guaranteed; the question is what you choose to miss.

You realise something quieter and more durable: **not everything must be done, but something must be done well.**

That realisation doesn't remove grief or fear. It doesn't make loss painless. It doesn't explain suffering.

What it does is relocate attention—away from the fantasy of total control and toward the reality of limited time.

You stop trying to do everything and start choosing something. You stop deferring what matters and start acting on it. You stop treating the present as preparation for a more critical future and recognise it as the only time you actually have.

Under the sun, death comes to everyone.

The wise and the foolish both die. The righteous and the wicked both die. Memory fades. Legacies erode. Even the most significant achievements eventually dissolve into history's background noise.

This is not nihilism. It is realism.

And, paradoxically, realism is what makes choice meaningful. If time were infinite, nothing would be urgent. If life never ended, presence would be optional. If death weren't real, the present could always be postponed.

But it can't be.

The question is not whether life ends.
The question is whether we live as though it does.

Chapter 10: Why Small Mistakes Wreck Big Lives

Most lives don't collapse all at once.

They tilt.

A comment was not corrected.
A habit indulged.
A warning ignored.
A shortcut taken "just this once."

Nothing dramatic happens. Nothing that would justify alarm. Life continues, essentially unchanged. From the outside, everything still looks intact.

That's what makes small mistakes so dangerous.

John worked in finance for fifteen years. Solid reputation. Respected by colleagues. Never the flashiest performer, but reliable, ethical, thorough.

Then the pressure increased. Quarterly targets tightened. Competitors were cutting corners—nothing illegal exactly, but aggressive. His boss started asking questions about why their numbers lagged.

So, John made a slight adjustment. He reclassified one expense to make the quarterly report look slightly better. The amount was trivial—less than 1% of the budget. No one would notice. It wasn't fraud exactly, just... creative accounting. Standard practice, really.

Nothing happened.

Three months later, he did it again. Slightly larger amount this time. Still well within the grey zone. Still justifiable if anyone asked—which they wouldn't.

Then it became routine. The quarterly scramble. The small adjustments. The "this won't matter" reasoning that made each decision feel isolated rather than part of a pattern.

Five years later, an audit revealed systematic misclassification. Not dramatic fraud—just consistent, incremental manipulation. His career ended not with a bang but with a memo. "Terminated for cause."

When colleagues asked how it happened, he genuinely couldn't explain. He'd never intended to build a pattern. Each decision had felt minor, defensible, separate from the others.

But they weren't separate. They were cumulative.

And cumulative is how lives tilt.

We tend to fear catastrophe—sudden failure, public disgrace, obvious disaster. But catastrophe is rare. What's common is drift. **Direction changes slowly, invisibly, until one day the distance travelled becomes undeniable.**

By then, the momentum is difficult to reverse.

This is why people often say, "I don't know how I ended up here." They didn't suddenly end up anywhere. They arrived incrementally.

Small decisions compound because life is cumulative. Behaviour repeats. Habits harden. Patterns stabilise. Over time, what once felt insignificant becomes structural.

This is not about moral weakness.
It's about scale.

Human beings are not especially good at perceiving long-term consequences. We respond to immediate feedback, not distant outcomes. A small gain now feels more real than a significant loss later. Behavioural economists call this temporal discounting—the robust human tendency to prioritise short-term relief over long-term outcomes.[1]

The mechanism is straightforward: our brains discount future consequences exponentially. A problem twenty years away feels abstract, almost theoretical. A problem five years away feels distant but real. A problem next month feels urgent. A problem today feels critical.

This means we consistently undervalue the future impact of present choices. The expense we put on the credit card "just this once" feels minor compared to the abstract burden of accumulating debt. The difficult conversation we postponed feels like relief now, rather than the vague possibility of relationship damage later. The health warning we ignore feels like freedom today, rather than the theoretical risk of disease someday.

Each choice in isolation seems rational. The immediate benefit is tangible. The future cost is speculative.

So, we delay the difficult conversation.
We excuse the minor compromise.
We tolerate the habit that isn't hurting anyone—yet.

And because nothing collapses immediately, we assume nothing serious is happening.

This is folly's advantage.

Folly does not announce itself as danger. It presents itself as convenience, relief, or common sense. It rarely asks for much upfront. It asks only to be left unchallenged.

History is full of examples where minor misjudgements produced outsized consequences.

Organisations fail not because of a single disastrous decision, but because of repeated minor evasions. Enron didn't collapse from a single act of fraud—it collapsed from a culture that normalised incremental deception until the gap between appearance and reality became unbridgeable.

Relationships fracture not from a single betrayal, but from accumulated neglect. The marriage doesn't end the day someone forgets an anniversary. It ends after a thousand small moments of inattention compound into estrangement.

Careers derail not from incompetence, but from reputation erosion—one overlooked detail at a time. The promotion doesn't go to the person who made one big mistake. It goes to someone else because of a pattern of small ones that signalled unreliability.

What makes this especially unsettling is how often intelligence fails to prevent it.

People know better.
They notice the signs.
They even predict the outcome.

But **prediction is not prevention.**

Knowing that something is unwise does not automatically produce restraint. In fact, familiarity often dulls urgency. When risk becomes routine, it stops feeling risky.

This is why experienced people sometimes fall harder than novices. Familiarity breeds confidence, and confidence reduces caution. The pilot who's flown a thousand times stops checking every gauge as carefully. The surgeon who has performed a procedure repeatedly becomes less vigilant about protocol. The driver who knows the route stops paying full attention.

The very experience that should protect them can make them brittle.

Diane Vaughan's landmark study of the Challenger disaster revealed how this happens systematically. NASA engineers had noticed O-ring erosion on previous shuttle flights. Each time, the shuttle returned safely despite the erosion. Gradually, what should have been alarming became normal. Concern was documented, discussed, and then... accepted.[2]

Standards quietly adjusted. The definition of "acceptable risk" crept upward. Small departures from engineering specifications became routine because nothing catastrophic happened immediately.

Until it did.

Seven astronauts died not because of ignorance or incompetence, but because of normalised deviance—the process by which small departures from best practice gradually become acceptable. Safety eroded quietly. Standards loosened slowly. Failure arrived late.

By the time it did, everyone insisted the outcome was unforeseeable.

It rarely is.

Small mistakes also thrive because they are easy to justify. They hide behind good intentions. They borrow legitimacy from context. They blend into the noise of everyday life.

No one says, "I am choosing a path that will ruin me."
They say, **"This won't matter."**

That phrase does more damage than almost any other.

Because it's often technically accurate—in isolation, any single instance of "this won't matter" is probably accurate. Missing one workout won't wreck your health. One harsh comment won't destroy a relationship. One credit card expense won't bankrupt you. One skipped safety check won't cause a disaster.

The problem is that "this won't matter" operates as a permission structure. Each instance validates the next. The phrase doesn't describe reality—it creates it by making repetition feel like isolated incidents rather than a pattern.

And patterns are what actually matter.

Because some things matter not by intensity, but by repetition.

A single missed boundary means little.
A pattern of them reshapes character.

A single lapse in attention is trivial.
A habit of inattention compounds.

A single ethical compromise feels survivable.
A series of them quietly rewrites who you are.

The person who cuts one corner doesn't become dishonest. But the person who repeatedly cuts corners does not undergo a dramatic moral collapse; instead, an incremental recalibration of what "acceptable" means. Each compromise makes the next one easier. The threshold shifts. The internal dialogue changes from "I shouldn't do this" to "Everyone does this" to "This is just how things work."

Character isn't destroyed in a moment. It erodes through a thousand small accommodations that each seemed reasonable at the time.

This is where fragility enters the picture.

Fragile systems appear strong until stress is applied. They function normally under ideal conditions, then fail disproportionately when disturbed. Human lives often work the same way. We appear resilient until accumulated strain finds the weak point.

And the weak point is rarely where we expected it.

Nassim Taleb's concept of fragility helps explain why: small stresses that are individually manageable can accumulate to create hidden vulnerability.[3] The system—whether organisational, relational, or personal—looks fine because it hasn't been tested. But the margin has disappeared.

Margin is the difference between what you can handle and what you're currently handling. It's a financial buffer, an emotional reserve, relational goodwill, physical health, and reputational credit. Margin is what allows you to absorb shocks, recover from mistakes, and endure hardship.

And the margin disappears gradually.

Each small compromise reduces it slightly. Each postponed maintenance task narrows it. Each tolerated bad habit eats into it. None of these feels significant because the system still functions. But resilience is quietly being converted into rigidity.

Then stress arrives—a health crisis, a market downturn, a relationship conflict, a professional challenge. Something that would have been manageable with a margin becomes catastrophic without it. The system that appeared strong proves brittle.

The unsettling truth is that small mistakes don't just cause enormous consequences—they create significant vulnerabilities. They narrow options. They reduce flexibility. They make recovery more complicated.

Over time, the margin disappears.

This is why people in crisis often say, "If I could go back, I would have taken it more seriously." They don't mean the final failure. They mean the earlier moments that seemed too minor to address.

Moments of inattention.
Moments of avoidance.
Moments of quiet compromise.

None of these felt decisive at the time.
That's the point.

Modern culture struggles with this idea because it prefers dramatic narratives. We like villains, turning points, and clear causes. Minor mistakes don't fit the story. They're boring. They lack spectacle.

But reality is not obligated to be interesting.

Under the sun, most damage is done gradually, by forces too ordinary to fear.

The perfumer's precious ointment doesn't require a catastrophic contamination to be ruined. Just a few dead flies. Just a small amount of decay was introduced into something otherwise valuable. The proportion seems absurd—how can something so minor ruin something so significant?

But it does.

A little folly outweighs wisdom and honour, not because folly is powerful, but because integrity is fragile. Reputation takes years to build and moments to destroy. Trust accumulates slowly and evaporates quickly. Health is maintained through consistent attention and lost through consistent neglect.

This is not meant to produce anxiety. It is meant to restore proportion.

When you understand how fragility works, you stop looking for dramatic threats and start paying attention to direction. You stop asking only whether something is permissible and start asking whether it is forming a pattern.

You begin to respect small decisions again.

Not because they are catastrophic—but because they are cumulative.

Folly is rarely loud.
It is patient.

It doesn't demand immediate surrender. It simply requests permission to stay. And if you grant that permission often enough, it stops asking for it.

Wisdom, such as it is, does not eliminate error. It reduces exposure. It keeps margins intact. It recognises that life does not require perfection—but it does require attention.

Attention to pattern, not just incident.
Attention to direction, not just destination.
Pay attention to small things before they compound into large ones.

This means correcting the comment when it's still minor. Addressing the habit before it hardens. Acting on the warning before it becomes prophecy. Refusing the shortcut when it's still just "this once."

Not because any single instance is catastrophic.
Because patterns determine trajectories.

Under the sun, big lives are rarely ruined by one terrible mistake.

They are undone by many small ones left unexamined.

Chapter 11: Why Risk Is the Price of Meaning

After enough illusions fall away, a quiet question remains.

If success doesn't settle the soul,
If progress repeats itself,
If pleasure fades,
If work can't define us,
If fairness isn't guaranteed,
If money can't secure us,
If intelligence doesn't save us,
If power rewards the wrong people,
If time runs out,
and if small mistakes accumulate quietly—

Then what is left to do?

This is the point where some people expect relief. Others expect despair. What usually arrives instead is something more unsettling: responsibility.

Not the kind imposed by rules or expectations, but the kind that remains when guarantees are gone.

Because once you stop believing life will reward you fairly, protect you reliably, or explain itself clearly, you are left with a choice that cannot be outsourced.

You still have to decide how to live.

Meaning does not disappear when illusions collapse.
It becomes riskier.

Sarah had always wanted children. But after years of trying, multiple miscarriages, and failed fertility treatments, she and her husband faced a decision: pursue adoption, knowing it would be expensive, emotionally gruelling, and uncertain, or accept being childless.

There were no guarantees with adoption. The process could take years. It could fall through at the last moment. The child might have trauma, medical needs, or attachment difficulties. The cost—financial and emotional—was substantial. And there was always the possibility that after all of it, nothing would work out.

A rational risk assessment would have advised against it.

But Sarah wasn't making a rational calculation. She was choosing what mattered enough to risk disappointment.

They pursued adoption.

The process took three years. There were false starts. There was heartbreak. There were moments when they wanted to quit. And eventually, they brought home a daughter from foster care—a five-year-old with a history of neglect and developmental delays.

The first two years were brutal. Tantrums. Attachment issues. Therapeutic interventions. Moments when Sarah wondered if she'd made a terrible mistake.

Ten years later, she still doesn't know if it was the "right" decision in any objective sense. Her daughter still struggles. The relationship is still complicated. No, Hollywood ends with everything resolving beautifully.

But she doesn't regret it.

Not because it worked out perfectly—it didn't. But choosing to love this child, despite the uncertainty and difficulty, was meaningful in a way that safety never would have been.

She risked herself for something that mattered. And that choice, independent of outcomes, was right.

This is where many people hesitate.

They have spent years constructing lives designed to minimise exposure to loss, embarrassment, rejection, and regret. They have learned to hedge emotionally, professionally, and relationally. They have mistaken caution for wisdom and control for maturity.

And it has worked—up to a point.

Hedging protects against catastrophic loss. It diversifies risk. It prevents single points of failure. In finance, this is prudent. In life, it creates a different problem.

When you hedge everything, you commit fully to nothing. You date without investing deeply. You work without caring too much. You build friendships with emotional escape clauses. You pursue goals with one eye on the exit.

The logic is understandable: if you don't risk much, you can't lose much.

But the corollary is equally true: if you don't risk much, you can't *gain* much either. Not in the things that matter most.

Safety has a ceiling.
Beyond it lies stagnation.

You can build a perfectly risk-managed life—financially stable, socially acceptable, emotionally insulated—and still feel a quiet, persistent emptiness. Not because you failed, but because you succeeded at the wrong thing. You optimised for safety when what you actually needed was meaning.

And meaning doesn't do safety.

Research by Laura King and Joshua Hicks demonstrates that meaning is most strongly associated not with comfort or predictability, but with commitment to values that involve uncertainty and cost.[1] Relationships, creative work, moral action, and generosity—all require vulnerability. All involve the possibility of loss.

Meaning does not emerge from risk avoidance.
It emerges from chosen risk.

This is not reckless risk—the thrill-seeking kind that confuses danger with aliveness, that pursues adrenaline for its own sake, that mistakes motion for meaning.

Reckless risk is impulsive. It chases novelty. It's performed for others. It confuses intensity with significance. Skydiving, extreme sports, casual affairs, and financial gambling—these can provide excitement but rarely provide meaning. They're often distractions from meaning, not paths to it.

Meaningful risk is different.

It's the quieter, riskier act of acting without assurance of an outcome.

Speaking honestly when silence would be safer.
Caring deeply when detachment would hurt less.
Building something without knowing whether it will last.
Loving someone without guarantees.
Pursuing work that matters despite no promise of recognition.
Standing for something even when it costs you.

These choices do not promise success. They promise exposure.

Which is precisely why they matter.

Meaningful risk is tethered to values that survive disappointment. It persists even when outcomes disappoint. It doesn't rely on applause, permanence, or success to validate the choice.

You pursue the work because the work itself matters, not because it will make you famous. You love the person because they're worth loving, not because they'll never leave. You speak the truth because it's true, not because it will be received well. You create because creation is meaningful, not because the market will reward it.

The value exists in the commitment itself, not in guaranteed outcomes.

This is why meaning can coexist with failure.

Viktor Frankl, writing from his experience in Nazi concentration camps, established that meaning emerges through responsibility and choice even when control over outcomes is absent.[2] Prisoners who found meaning—through caring for others, maintaining dignity, choosing how to respond—survived psychological collapse better than those who didn't. Not because meaning guaranteed survival, but because meaning sustained the will to live regardless of outcomes.

You can fail at what matters and still have lived rightly.
You can lose what mattered and still be right to love it.
You can take the risk and pay the price—and not regret it.

That logic makes no sense in a world obsessed with outcomes. We're trained to evaluate decisions by results.

Good outcome = good decision.

Bad outcome = bad decision.

But that's not how meaning works.

Choosing to love someone who later left you wasn't wrong; they left.
Creating work that fails commercially wasn't foolish because it failed.
Fighting for a cause that was lost wasn't pointless because it was lost.

The rightness existed in the choice itself—in the willingness to care about something beyond yourself, to commit despite uncertainty, to act according to what mattered rather than what was guaranteed.

Outcomes were never entirely under your control, anyway.

What *is* yours to control is whether you risk yourself for what matters or retreat into safety and call it wisdom.

If meaning were safe, it would be trivial.
If it were guaranteed, it would be cheap.
If it were controllable, it would be hollow.

The desire for meaning without risk is understandable—but it is also impossible. **Risk is not a flaw in the system. It is the entry fee.**

This is where many modern strategies for living quietly fail. They aim for a life that is manageable, optimised, and insulated. They remove friction wherever possible. Productivity systems promise control. Self-help promises formulas. Therapy promises emotional safety. Insurance promises protection.

None of these is bad. But when the goal becomes a life free of risk, something essential gets eliminated along with the danger.

A life without risk may feel stable, but it rarely feels significant.

Research distinguishes meaning from happiness precisely along this line: happy lives correlate with comfort and need-satisfaction; meaningful lives often involve stress, effort, sacrifice, and concern for others.[3] Happiness avoids difficulty. Meaning engages it willingly when something important is at stake.

And yet—this is important—**risk does not mean chaos.**

It means choosing where uncertainty is worth it.

Not every risk matters.
Not every gamble is meaningful.
Some risks are distractions dressed up as courage.

The question is not "Am I taking risks?" but "What am I risking myself for, and does it survive disappointment?"

If the answer is ego, novelty, or proving something to others—that's not meaningful risk. That's performance. And performance doesn't survive failure.

But if the answer is love, truth, creation, justice, beauty, or connection—things that matter independent of outcomes—then risk becomes meaningful. It becomes the vehicle through which you participate in what matters rather than observe it.

Here is where the subtitle begins to breathe:

**If nothing matters in the way we were promised—
if nothing guarantees us significance, security, or permanence—**

Then the pressure lifts.

This is the paradox at the heart of it all.

When you accept that success won't settle your soul, that progress repeats, that pleasure fades, that work can't define you, that fairness isn't guaranteed, that money can't secure you, that intelligence doesn't save you, that power rewards the wrong people, that time runs out, and that small mistakes compound—

You are no longer required to win at life.

You are no longer required to justify your existence through results.

You are no longer required to eliminate uncertainty before acting.

You are no longer required to make every choice pay off.

You are free to choose what is worth risking yourself for.

This is what **"that's okay"** actually means.

Not resignation—the defeated acceptance that nothing can be done.
Not apathy—the indifference that nothing is worth caring about.
Not indifference—the coldness that protects against disappointment.

It means **permission to live without insurance against disappointment.**

When you stop demanding that life reward you, protect you, or explain itself, you discover something unexpected: you're free to act anyway. Free to care without guarantee. Free to build without permanence. Free to love without security.

The illusions that collapsed weren't supporting you. They were pressuring you.

They were demanding you prove your worth through success, accumulate enough to feel safe, understand enough to control outcomes, and achieve enough to matter. They were insisting that meaning must be earned, secured, and validated by results.

But meaning doesn't work that way.

When meaning is chosen rather than secured, it becomes resilient. It can survive loss. It can coexist with doubt. It does not collapse when things go wrong.

This is why people often discover meaning not at the peak of certainty, but at the edge of it—when something important is at stake, and nothing guarantees it will work out.

Parents find meaning in raising children, even when they don't know how they'll turn out.
Artists find meaning in creating despite not knowing if anyone will care.
Activists find meaning in working for change, even when they don't know if they'll succeed.
Lovers find meaning in commitment despite not knowing if it will last.

The uncertainty isn't incidental. It's intrinsic.

If the outcome were guaranteed, the choice would be calculation, not commitment. If success were assured, the act would be an investment, not a risk. If loss were impossible, love would be strategy, not vulnerability.

Meaning lives precisely in the gap between action and outcome—in the willingness to commit despite not knowing, to care despite potential loss, to act despite uncertainty.

Under the sun, no choice is protected from loss.

Everything you build will eventually erode. Everyone you love will eventually die or leave. Every achievement will eventually be forgotten. Every certainty will eventually be questioned.

This is not pessimism. This is realism.

And realism, strangely, is what makes choice meaningful.

But some choices are worth making anyway.

Not because they promise success.
Not because they guarantee significance.
Not because they protect against loss.

But because they participate in what matters—now, in this moment, with whatever limited time and uncertain outcomes you have.

Meaning lives there—not in outcomes, not in permanence, not in safety—**but in the willingness to risk yourself for something that may not last, may fail, and may not be remembered.**

And that is not tragic.

That is human.

Chapter 12: Living Well Without Illusions

Eventually, every serious person arrives at the same place.

Not all at once.
Not by the same route.
But unmistakably.

The place where illusions stop being useful.

Some illusions collapse under pressure. Others wear out. What once motivated begins to feel thin. What once promised clarity begins to feel loud. The stories that carried us through earlier seasons no longer fit the weight of experience.

This is not failure.
It is an arrival.

Michael Epstein reached this place at 52, after a decade-long career pivot that didn't work out the way he'd hoped. He'd left a stable corporate job to start a nonprofit addressing homelessness—work that mattered to him deeply. He'd raised money, built programs, and hired staff. For five years, it grew.

Then funding dried up. Key partnerships fell through, perhaps because Michael's surname was mistaken for shared kinship with *Jeffrey Epstein.* The organisation limped along for another five years before he finally had to shut it down.

By conventional metrics, he'd failed. A decade of his life produced an entity that no longer existed. The impact he'd hoped to make was smaller than he'd imagined. The legacy he'd envisioned didn't materialise.

But when I asked if he regretted it, he said something unexpected: "No. I don't need it to have been more than it was."

He'd stopped requiring the work to justify the decade. Stopped needing the outcome to validate the choice. Stopped demanding that effort equal lasting achievement.

He'd done work that mattered for as long as he could, and then it ended.

And he was okay.

Not because he'd learned to lower his standards or settle for less. But because he'd stopped organising his life around the wrong ultimate value.

Living well without illusions does not mean living without hope. It means living without false expectations. It means releasing the demand that life justify itself, explain itself, or reward itself on our terms.

By this point, much has already fallen away.

Success has been demoted.
Progress has been questioned.
Pleasure has been exposed.
Productivity has been unmasked.
Fairness has been relinquished.
Money, intelligence, and power have been stripped of their false authority.
Time has been acknowledged.
Fragility has been respected.
Risk has been embraced.

What remains is nothing.

What remains is life, as it is.

Limited.
Unfinished.
Unsecured.

And still worth living.

This is where many people make a final mistake. Having lost their illusions, they assume they must now live cautiously, quietly, defensively—as though wisdom were a form of retreat.

It isn't.

Living without illusions does not shrink life. It clarifies it.

When you stop expecting permanence, you stop clinging.
When you stop demanding fairness, you stop bargaining.
When you stop waiting for certainty, you stop postponing.

Attention returns.
Ordinary moments regain weight.

Relationships matter again—not because they last forever, but because they don't. The temporary nature of the connection makes presence all the more urgent. The meal with your ageing parent isn't preparation for future meals. It's this meal. The conversation with your child isn't building toward some climactic moment of understanding. It's this conversation.

Work finds its proper scale. It's no longer tasked with providing identity, purpose, and validation. It's work—sometimes meaningful, sometimes tedious, always finite. You can do it well without needing it to complete you.

Enjoyment becomes simpler. You don't need experience to appreciate them; you need to be exceptional. The coffee is just coffee, but you notice it. The walk is just a walk, but you're actually there. Pleasure returns to appropriate proportions—a feature of life, not its purpose.

Responsibility becomes quieter and more honest. You act rightly not because it guarantees reward but because right action has its own integrity. You keep commitments not because they'll be recognised but because keeping them matters regardless of recognition.

You no longer need life to be exceptional in order for it to be sufficient.

This is the freedom most people are looking for without knowing how to name it.

The freedom from proving.
The freedom from performing.
The freedom from needing everything to matter equally.

Because when everything matters, nothing does.

Living well without illusions means learning to live selectively. Choosing where to give attention. Choosing what to care about. Choosing what to release.

Research on wisdom consistently shows that it involves not just accumulated knowledge but discernment about what deserves focus and what doesn't. Wise people don't try to optimise everything. They accept that some things will remain imperfect, some questions will remain unanswered, and some efforts will remain incomplete.[1]

This selectivity requires knowing what you're selecting *for*—what ultimate framework you're living by.

Everyone operates according to some ultimate value, whether they've examined it consciously or not. Some organise their lives around transcendent realities—God, ultimate truth, cosmic order. Others around ideological commitments—progress, justice, reason, human flourishing. Still others are around relationships—family, community, roles that define identity.

These function similarly regardless of what you call them. They answer the fundamental questions: *What makes life meaningful? What am I accountable to? What is worth sacrificing for?*

The illusions this book has been dismantling are often disguised versions of these ultimate values, asked to bear weight they cannot sustain.

Success won't ultimately satisfy—not because achievement is worthless, but because it's finite.

Progress won't perfect the world—not because improvement is impossible, but because patterns repeat.
Relationships won't complete you—not because connection doesn't matter, but because people are as limited as you are.
Reason won't save you—not because intelligence is useless, but because understanding doesn't equal control.

Everything under the sun is finite. And finite things cannot bear infinite weight.

It means accepting that some questions will remain unanswered. Why do the righteous suffer? Why does injustice persist? Why does time move in only one direction? These aren't puzzles waiting for cleverer solutions. They're features of existence under the sun.

Some efforts will go unnoticed. Work you pour yourself into will be forgotten. Sacrifices you make won't be acknowledged. Contributions you believe are significant will dissolve into history's background noise.

Some losses will never make sense. People die too young. Relationships end without closure. Potential goes unrealised. And no amount of reflection will force sense into senselessness.

Some endings will arrive without resolution. Projects will be interrupted. Goals will be abandoned. Stories will conclude mid-sentence.

And still choosing to live with care.

This is not a resignation.
It is maturity.

There is a particular peace that comes from finally agreeing with reality instead of arguing with it. From aligning expectations with the way things actually work. From letting go of the fantasy that life owes us coherence.

Under the sun, it does not.

What it offers instead is something quieter and more durable: **the chance to live honestly within limits.**

To enjoy what is given without demanding more.
To work without worshipping outcomes.
To love without insisting on guarantees.
To act rightly without expecting reward.
To accept risk without despair.
To face time without denial.

This is what remains when illusions are gone.

Not a system.
Not a formula.
Not a conclusion.

A posture.

This book has been working from a particular source code—one that explored these same tensions nearly three thousand years ago and arrived at a conclusion that has survived precisely because it doesn't pretend to solve what cannot be solved. The pattern you've been reading—the systematic dismantling of false sources of meaning under the sun—follows an ancient template. That template doesn't end with comfortable platitudes or self-help formulas. It ends with something more demanding and more honest.

It locates ultimate accountability beyond the closed system of human perception and temporal existence.[2] It insists that living well requires acknowledging something larger than yourself, submitting to standards you didn't create, and accepting that your perception isn't final.

Different readers will find "something larger" in different places.

Some will recognise divine authority—God, however understood within their tradition. The framework of ultimate accountability to a transcendent reality that defines meaning, establishes morality, and judges actions.

Others will translate into secular terms—reason itself, ethical truth, human dignity, the arc of justice—principles that transcend individual preference and demand alignment regardless of personal cost or outcome.

Still others will resist any framework of ultimate accountability, insisting that meaning can be constructed, ethics negotiated, and standards chosen without reference to anything beyond human agreement.

All three responses are honest.

What you cannot do is pretend you're operating without *some* ultimate framework. You are. Everyone is. The question is whether you've examined it consciously, whether it's adequate to bear the weight you're placing on it, and whether you're willing to be honest about its limitations.

The source code this book draws from insists that ultimate accountability must be located beyond what we can control or comprehend "under the sun." That our perception of fairness is not final. That our frustration with injustice is not the last word. That our inability to secure meaning does not mean meaning doesn't exist.

You don't have to accept that conclusion to benefit from everything that came before it. The observations stand on their own: success doesn't settle the soul, fairness isn't guaranteed, time runs out, and meaning requires risk.

But thousands of years of lived experience suggest that acknowledging accountability beyond yourself produces a particular kind of freedom.

The freedom to act rightly without controlling outcomes—because outcomes aren't the final verdict.
The freedom to love without guaranteeing returns—because the act of loving has worth beyond reciprocation.
The freedom to work without demanding vindication—because

vindication isn't required for the work to matter.
The freedom to face limits without despair—because limits aren't the end of the story.

Whether you locate that accountability in transcendent reality, universal principles, or something else, the structure remains the same: living well requires acknowledging something larger than yourself.

Living well without illusions does not make life safe.
It makes it real.

And reality, once accepted, turns out to be surprisingly livable.

Nothing matters in the way we were promised.

Success won't settle your soul.
Progress won't perfect the world.
Pleasure won't sustain you.
Work won't define you.
Fairness won't be guaranteed.
Money won't secure you.
Intelligence won't save you.
Power will reward the wrong people.
Time will run out.
Mistakes will compound.

And once you see that clearly, you may discover something unexpected:

That's okay.

Not because these realisations don't matter—they do. But because they clear space for what does matter to emerge without distortion.

When you stop demanding that finite things provide infinite meaning, they return to their proper proportions. Work becomes work again, not worship. Relationships become connections, not salvation. Success becomes pleasant, not sacred. Pleasure becomes enjoyable, not necessary.

And you become free to choose what's worth risking yourself for—not because it's guaranteed to work out, but because some things are worth doing even when outcomes are uncertain.

Under the sun, this is enough.

And beyond the sun—for those willing to look—there's an accountability that makes the limits bearable, a standard that makes choices meaningful, a judgment that makes integrity matter.

Whether you call that God, or something else entirely, the question remains the same:

How will you live within your limits?
What will you risk yourself for?
Who will you become when guarantees are gone?

The illusions are finished.

The living begins now.

Endnotes

Chapter 1: Why Success Doesn't Settle the Soul

[1] Philip Brickman and Donald T. Campbell, "Hedonic Relativism and Planning the Good Society," in *Adaptation-Level Theory*, ed. Mortimer H. Appley (New York: Academic Press, 1971), 287–305. See also Sonja Lyubomirsky, *The How of Happiness: A Scientific Approach to Getting the Life You Want* (New York: Penguin Press, 2008), particularly her discussion of the "hedonic treadmill" in achievement contexts and the distinction between baseline happiness and circumstantial satisfaction spikes.

Chapter 2: Why "Progress" Keeps Repeating Itself

[1] Neil Postman, *Technopoly: The Surrender of Culture to Technology* (New York: Vintage, 1993), 18-29. Postman argues that technology optimises and amplifies pre-existing human impulses rather than creating fundamentally new behaviours. See also Sherry Turkle, *Alone Together: Why We Expect More from Technology and Less from Each Other* (New York: Basic Books, 2011), 153-179, for longitudinal research demonstrating that digital platforms consistently scale existing social tendencies.

[2] Barry Schwartz, *The Paradox of Choice: Why More Is Less* (New York: Ecco, 2004), particularly chapter 5 on the relationship between choice abundance and life satisfaction. For longitudinal data on rising anxiety despite material improvements, see Jean M. Twenge, "The Age of Anxiety? The Birth Cohort Change in Anxiety and Neuroticism, 1952-1993," *Journal of Personality and Social Psychology* 79, no. 6 (2000): 1007-1021.

Chapter 3: Why Chasing Pleasure Never Works for Long

[1] Kent C. Berridge and Terry E. Robinson, "Liking, Wanting, and the Incentive-Sensitisation Theory of Addiction," *American Psychologist* 71, no. 8 (2016): 670-679. This research distinguishes dopamine's role in anticipation ("wanting") from its role in actual enjoyment ("liking"), and explains why pleasure responses diminish with repetition even as the desire for them may intensify—a dynamic central to understanding why chasing pleasure produces diminishing returns.

[2] Daniel Kahneman and Angus Deaton, "High Income Improves Evaluation of Life but Not Emotional Well-Being," *Proceedings of the National Academy of Sciences* 107, no. 38 (2010): 16489-16493. Demonstrates that beyond approximately

$75,000 annual income (in 2010 dollars), increased wealth and associated pleasures produce diminishing returns for day-to-day emotional well-being, while meaning-based satisfaction proves more durable and less subject to adaptation.

[3] Philip Brickman and Donald T. Campbell, "Hedonic Relativism and Planning the Good Society," in *Adaptation-Level Theory*, ed. Mortimer H. Appley (New York: Academic Press, 1971), 287-305. Foundational work establishing the hedonic adaptation principle—that humans return to a relatively stable baseline of happiness regardless of positive or negative changes in external circumstances. This explains why pursuing pleasure through accumulation or escalation rarely produces lasting satisfaction.

Chapter 4: The Lie of Productivity as Identity

[1] Richard Sennett, *The Corrosion of Character: The Personal Consequences of Work in the New Capitalism* (New York: W.W. Norton, 1998), 9-31. Sennett documents how flexible capitalism and post-industrial work culture have fundamentally reshaped identity formation, shifting work from "what you do" to "who you are"—a transformation that erodes long-term meaning, stability, and character development. His analysis demonstrates how the demand for constant adaptability and availability corrodes the capacity to build coherent narratives of self.

[2] Christina Maslach and Michael P. Leiter, "Understanding the Burnout Experience: Recent Research and Its Implications for Psychiatry," *World Psychiatry* 15, no. 2 (2016): 103-111. This research links burnout specifically to identity fusion with work roles and demonstrates that over-identification with productivity correlates strongly with anxiety, depression, and chronic emotional exhaustion. The problem is not hard work per se, but the collapse of boundaries between self-worth and occupational output.

Chapter 5: Why Fairness Is Not Guaranteed

[1] Robert H. Frank, *Success and Luck: Good Fortune and the Myth of Meritocracy* (Princeton: Princeton University Press, 2016), 34-58. Frank demonstrates that societies emphasising meritocratic narratives—where success is attributed primarily to individual talent and effort—paradoxically generate more resentment and social division. When outcomes are framed as purely "earned," inequality feels like a personal moral verdict rather than a product of circumstance, luck, and structural factors. This intensifies envy and corrodes social cohesion.

[2] Richard Wilkinson and Kate Pickett, *The Spirit Level: Why Greater Equality Makes Societies Stronger* (New York: Bloomsbury Press, 2009), 52-87. Their comprehensive analysis of developed nations demonstrates that relative inequality erodes social trust, well-being, and cohesion far more powerfully than absolute poverty levels. Persistent unfairness—not mere hardship—corrodes the social fabric by teaching people that cooperation is futile and the system is rigged against them.

Chapter 6: Why Money Can't Make You Feel Secure

[1] Daniel Kahneman and Angus Deaton, "High Income Improves Evaluation of Life but Not Emotional Well-Being," *Proceedings of the National Academy of Sciences* 107, no. 38 (2010): 16489-16493. Their research demonstrates that beyond approximately $75,000 annual income (in 2010 dollars), additional money produces sharply diminishing emotional returns. While higher income continues to improve life evaluation (how people think about their lives cognitively), it does little to reduce day-to-day anxiety or increase moment-to-moment happiness—revealing the crucial distinction between comfort and genuine security.

[2] Richard Wilkinson and Kate Pickett, *The Spirit Level: Why Greater Equality Makes Societies Stronger* (New York: Bloomsbury Press, 2009), 35-52. Their analysis explores how status anxiety—the fear of falling behind in relative social position—intensifies in high-income but unequal societies. Even objectively wealthy individuals experience chronic insecurity when surrounded by visible inequality, as money becomes a scoreboard for social worth rather than simply a resource for meeting needs.

[3] Robert H. Frank, *Falling Behind: How Rising Inequality Harms the Middle Class* (Stanford: Stanford University Press, 2007), 18-45. Frank details how relative income comparisons intensify financial insecurity even amid overall wealth growth. As reference groups shift upward—through social media visibility, geographic sorting, and professional networks—what feels like "enough" constantly escalates, creating a treadmill of anxiety that no absolute level of income can satisfy.

Chapter 7: Why Intelligence Doesn't Save You

[1] Keith E. Stanovich and Richard F. West, "Individual Differences in Reasoning: Implications for the Rationality Debate," *Behavioural and Brain Sciences* 23, no. 5 (2000): 645-726. Their extensive research demonstrates that intelligence (as measured by IQ) does not reliably predict rational decision-making in real-world contexts, particularly under emotional pressure or when heuristics and biases are at play. Smart people excel at abstract reasoning and academic performance, but

not necessarily at self-regulation, judgment under uncertainty, or avoiding cognitive biases.

[2] Philip E. Tetlock, *Expert Political Judgment: How Good Is It? How Can We Know?* (Princeton: Princeton University Press, 2005). Tetlock's landmark 20-year study tracked 82,000 predictions by 284 experts across multiple domains and found that specialists performed no better than informed laypeople—and sometimes worse—in long-term forecasting. High intelligence and deep expertise did not translate to better prediction, revealing the limits of knowledge when facing irreducible uncertainty and complex systems.

[3] The observation that increased knowledge brings increased sorrow has deep historical roots, appearing prominently in Ecclesiastes 1:18: "For in much wisdom is much vexation, and he who increases knowledge increases sorrow." Modern psychology has confirmed this ancient insight: awareness of complexity, risk, and human limitations grows faster than our capacity to control outcomes, widening the gap between understanding and power. Intelligence illuminates problems it cannot solve.

Chapter 8: Why Power Rewards the Wrong People

[1] Dacher Keltner, *The Power Paradox: How We Gain and Lose Influence* (New York: Penguin Press, 2016), 89-124. Keltner's research demonstrates that the traits that help people gain power—assertiveness, confidence, strategic risk-taking, comfort with dominance—often erode the very capacities (empathy, ethical sensitivity, self-awareness, responsiveness to others) needed to use power responsibly. This creates a paradox: power selects for qualities that become liabilities once power is attained, explaining why those who rise are often least equipped to lead well.

[2] Robert Michels, *Political Parties: A Sociological Study of the Oligarchical Tendencies of Modern Democracy*, trans. Eden Paul and Cedar Paul (1911; repr., New York: Free Press, 1962), 342-356. Michels introduced the "iron law of oligarchy," arguing that all organisations—even those founded on democratic, egalitarian principles—inevitably drift toward concentrated power and institutional self-preservation at the expense of stated values. The system selects leaders who prioritise organisational survival over original ideals, not through conspiracy but through structural incentives.

[3] Cameron Anderson and Sebastien Brion, "Perspectives on Power in Organizations," *Annual Review of Organizational Psychology and Organizational Behaviour* 1 (2014): 67-97. Their comprehensive review documents how holding power systematically alters perceptions, risk assessments, and moral judgments. Power-holders overestimate their influence, underestimate risks, discount dissent, and

become less responsive to feedback—creating a dangerous insulation effect that compounds initial selection biases with ongoing perceptual distortion.

Chapter 9: The Problem No One Escapes

[1] Philippe Ariès, *Western Attitudes toward Death: From the Middle Ages to the Present*, trans. Patricia M. Ranum (Baltimore: Johns Hopkins University Press, 1974). Ariès traces how Western societies have progressively distanced themselves from death over several centuries—moving it from home to hospital, from family ritual to professional management, from public communal acknowledgement to private euphemism. Modern death is sanitised, medicalised, and hidden behind institutional walls, making it psychologically more challenging to integrate mortality as a natural boundary condition rather than a failure to be avoided.

[2] Ernest Becker, *The Denial of Death* (New York: Free Press, 1973), 11-58. Becker's Pulitzer Prize-winning work argues that much of human civilisation represents an elaborate symbolic system designed to manage the terror of mortality. People oscillate between denial (distraction, busyness, forgetting) and overcompensation (attempts to achieve symbolic immortality through legacy, achievement, or recognition). Both strategies avoid confrontation with finitude, which Becker sees as the central existential challenge of being human.

[3] Laura L. Carstensen, "The Influence of a Sense of Time on Human Development," *Science* 312, no. 5782 (2006): 1913-1915. Carstensen's socioemotional selectivity theory demonstrates that perceived time horizons fundamentally reshape priorities, emotional focus, and value systems. When people become aware that time is limited—through ageing, illness, or mortality salience—they narrow their focus toward emotionally meaningful goals: deepening relationships, savouring experiences, pursuing reconciliation, and making immediate contributions. Abstract long-term ambitions and status competition systematically weaken as time horizons shorten.

Chapter 10: Why Small Mistakes Wreck Big Lives

[1] Shane Frederick, George Loewenstein, and Ted O'Donoghue, "Time Discounting and Time Preference: A Critical Review," *Journal of Economic Literature* 40, no. 2 (2002): 351-401. This comprehensive review explains temporal discounting—the robust human tendency to prioritise short-term relief over long-term outcomes. People consistently undervalue future consequences relative to present comfort, making small immediate gains feel more real than significant delayed losses. This cognitive bias explains why we excuse minor compromises, tolerate the development of bad habits, and delay difficult but necessary actions, even when we intellectually understand the long-term costs.

[2] Diane Vaughan, *The Challenger Launch Decision: Risky Technology, Culture, and Deviance at NASA* (Chicago: University of Chicago Press, 1996), 77-120. Vaughan introduces the concept of "normalisation of deviance"—the process by which small departures from best practice gradually become acceptable because nothing bad happens immediately. Her analysis of the Challenger disaster reveals how organisations drift toward catastrophe through accumulated minor evasions rather than single catastrophic decisions. Safety erodes quietly; standards loosen slowly; failure arrives late. By the time disaster strikes, the deviation has become so normalised that the outcome genuinely seems unforeseeable—even though warning signs were documented throughout.

[3] Nassim Nicholas Taleb, *Antifragile: Things That Gain from Disorder* (New York: Random House, 2012), 44-89. Taleb explores how fragility accumulates invisibly in systems that appear strong under normal conditions but fail disproportionately when stressed. Minor accumulated strains create hidden vulnerabilities that sudden shocks expose. What appears resilient proves brittle because the margin—the buffer between current load and maximum capacity—has disappeared gradually and unnoticed. Fragile systems optimise for efficiency at the cost of resilience, leaving no room for error when conditions change.

Chapter 11: Why Risk Is the Price of Meaning

[1] Laura A. King and Joshua A. Hicks, "The Science of Meaning in Life," *Annual Review of Psychology* 72 (2021): 561-584. Their comprehensive review demonstrates that meaning is most strongly associated with commitment, responsibility, and value-driven action rather than comfort, pleasure, or predictability. Meaningful lives consistently involve uncertainty, effort, and cost—the willingness to be vulnerable to loss in service of what matters. People find meaning not through risk avoidance but through chosen engagement with what they value, even when outcomes are uncertain.

[2] Viktor E. Frankl, *Man's Search for Meaning* (1959; repr., Boston: Beacon Press, 2006), 65-106. Frankl's foundational work, written from his experience surviving Nazi concentration camps, establishes that meaning emerges through responsibility and choice even in the complete absence of control over outcomes. He observed that prisoners who found meaning—through caring for others, maintaining dignity, choosing their response to suffering—survived psychological collapse better than those who didn't. Freedom of choice persists even when all other freedoms are stripped away, and meaning arises from exercising that freedom responsibly, regardless of circumstances.

[3] Roy F. Baumeister, Kathleen D. Vohs, Jennifer L. Aaker, and Emily N. Garbinsky, "Some Key Differences between a Happy Life and a Meaningful Life,"

Journal of Positive Psychology 8, no. 6 (2013): 505-516. This research systematically distinguishes meaning from happiness, showing that meaningful lives often involve stress, effort, sacrifice, and concern for future consequences—dimensions that happy lives avoid. Happiness correlates with comfort, need-satisfaction, and present-focus; meaning correlates with commitment, contribution, and willingness to endure difficulty for what matters. The two can coexist, but they have different sources and costs.

Chapter 12: Living Well Without Illusions

[1] Judith Glück and Susan Bluck, "The MORE Life Experience Model: A Theory of the Development of Personal Wisdom," in *The Scientific Study of Personal Wisdom*, ed. Michel Ferrari and Nic M. Weststrate (Dordrecht: Springer, 2013), 75-97. Their research demonstrates that wisdom involves not just knowledge accumulation but the capacity for discernment—knowing what deserves attention and what can be released, what can be changed and what must be accepted. Wise individuals show greater comfort with ambiguity, paradox, and unresolved questions, suggesting that wisdom emerges not from eliminating uncertainty but from learning to live well within it.

[2] After observing that success, pleasure, wisdom, work, wealth, and power all fail to provide ultimate satisfaction, Ecclesiastes arrives at a conclusion that has endured for three millennia: "The end of the matter; all has been heard. Fear God and keep his commandments, for this is the whole duty of man. For God will bring every deed into judgment, with every secret thing, whether good or evil" (Ecclesiastes 12:13-14). This conclusion locates ultimate accountability beyond human perception—an accountability that makes choices meaningful even when outcomes are uncertain. Different readers will interpret "Fear God" differently: some as literal divine authority, others as reverence for that which transcends individual preference, and still others as submission to ethical truth or ultimate reality. The structure remains: living well requires acknowledging something larger than yourself, whatever you understand that to be.

Under the Hood

Some readers may notice patterns running beneath the surface of this book—recurring themes of repetition, limits, work, pleasure, injustice, time, and mortality.

That's intentional.

The structural backbone of this book draws inspiration from an ancient work of wisdom literature traditionally known as Ecclesiastes in the Bible. Rather than quoting or teaching from it directly, the aim here was to explore whether its observations still hold when translated into contemporary language and experience.

The experiment was simple:

Redact the religious framing, keep the human questions, and see what remains.

What emerged was not a set of answers, but a posture—one shaped by realism, restraint, and a refusal to pretend that life attainable parameters offer guarantees it never has.

Readers do not need familiarity with Ecclesiastes to engage with this book. The chapters are designed to stand nonetheless. But for those who recognise the lineage, the connections are there quietly, thematically chapter by chapter, like source code running beneath the user interface.

Nothing in this book depends on agreement.

It only asks for attention.

About the Author

Aham Igbokwe brings unique perspectives to questions of meaning, systems, and human limitations—shaped by decades navigating both corporate power structures and pastoral care.

A cybersecurity consultant, he has spent decades working across Fortune 20 companies advising on enterprise security architecture and technology transformations in sectors where minor errors compound into catastrophic failures and where intelligence alone cannot prevent human breakdown. He holds an MBA and an MA in Theology & Leadership from the University of Roehampton, London and multiple certifications, including CISSP, CISM, CISA, and CAISS (Certified AI Security Specialist).

A bi-vocational pastor and a Justice of the Peace for England & Wales, these vantage points—observing human systems through the judiciary, structural analysis, and spiritual care—shape his clear-eyed realism about what works under the sun and what doesn't. His writings examine perennial human questions through the lens of ancient wisdom and contemporary research, refusing both therapeutic oversimplification and human religiosities.

He is also the author of *Madness Is Not Stupidity*, *Common Sense for Uncommon Times*, *In Remission,* and other works.

British-born of Igbo extraction, Aham lives in Berkshire, United Kingdom.

For permissions, subsidiary rights, or bulk orders:

ahamigbokwe@outlook.com
www.x.com/iampastoraham

www.ingramcontent.com/pod-product-compliance
Lightning Source LLC
LaVergne TN
LVHW051013080826
845145LV00009B/2600

* 9 7 8 1 9 1 8 5 1 8 1 0 8 *